This is more than a book; it's a compreh
the world of sensory and emotional con
Chris Lukehurst skillfully bridges the connection between
product sensorial experience and the powerful emotions it
evokes, providing a blueprint that is as invaluable for product
innovation as it is for impactful marketing. By understanding
how taste shapes consumer loyalty across diverse cultures,
readers can forge authentic connections with their target
market and build lasting brand affinity.

Bruno Olierhoek, founder and CEO Ubuntu Advisory
Consultancy, former chairman and MD, Nestlé, East and
Southern Africa

Tearing away the superficial ways of looking at food and
consumption, this book takes us to the world of emotions
that food and taste unlock - the memories they stir and the
memories they can create. Chris Lukehurst breaks down the
journey we traverse in a moment of taste and how important
it is for marketers to understand the sequencing, intensity and
nature of this emotional journey. He highlights the necessity to
immerse yourself in the experience of a consumer, considering
maps of beliefs, emotions and cultural nuances as you do so.
This book helps answer many questions but it also teaches us
what are the right questions to focus on and how to turn them
into a competitive advantage.

Asim Rifat, vice president and business executive officer
- Nestlé Nutrition Middle East and North Africa

We choose foods because of how they make us feel. This book and the work that Chris has spent a lifetime doing effectively demonstrate that connecting with consumers isn't just about taste; it's about creating an emotional journey.

Dr Mary Carunchia PhD, food scientist

Foods and beverages take us on an emotional journey that is important to understand for marketers. The Marketing Clinic method is able to map the sequencing, intensity, and nature of the journey to point out which tangible elements evoke these emotional experiences. Armed with this knowledge, marketers can create better products, diagnose reasons for dips and generate highly relevant positioning and advertising. In an era of increasing digitization, the TMC method is an outstanding example of the deep and enduring relevance of human insight.

Raji Bonala, director, qualitative research, Vox Populi Research, India

The Shape of Taste

Unraveling the **emotional journey** behind every mouthful and how it impacts your consumers

Chris Lukehurst

*For Caroline and our four sons—thank you for your love
and support in my work and my adventures.*

The Shape of Taste

ISBN 978-1-915483-84-3

eISBN 978-1-915483-85-0

Published in 2025 by Right Book Press

Printed in the UK in March 2025

Manufactured by
Sue Richardson Associates Ltd.
Studio 6,
9, Marsh Street
Bristol
BS1 4AA
info@therightbookcompany.com

EU Safety Representative
euComply OÜ
Parnu mnt 139b-14
11317 Tallinn
Estonia
hello@eucompliancepartner.com
+33 756 90241

Contents

Foreword: Martin Lindstrom   vii

Introduction   1
1 You are what you eat   9
2 The Shape of Taste   21
3 It's not about the best taste...   37
    it's about how it makes you feel
4 It's the journey that is the essence of the brand   47
5 How the Shape of Taste helps to improve   57
    communications and advertising
6 Diving deeper into complexity   71
7 Belief is vital   85
8 Creating new products that consumers will love   99
9 Cultural understanding is important...   109
    but cultures are not static
10 Telling stories that product owners may not   121
    want to hear
Afterword: The value of the Shape of Taste   129

Bibliography   133

Foreword

Martin Lindstrom

I first met Chris in Manila where we were introduced by a mutual client (now a mutual friend) for whom we were working on the same project at the same time. As we worked together, it quickly became apparent that while, at that time, we at Lindstrom Company were focusing upon consumer behavior and emotional responses, the work that Chris was doing at The Marketing Clinic, understanding how and why consumers' consumption experiences prompted those emotions, went a step further and was a great complement to our work.

Over the years since we first met, I have included Chris and his team in a number of our food and beverage projects where his particular set of skills and his knowledge and experience in food and beverage has added considerable value to our own work.

We traveled around Russia together (in those days before the invasion of Ukraine when such things were possible and business links were encouraged) researching the ideal vodka. Chris tells part of the story in Chapter 5 but omits to mention the fun we had and the deeply informative conversations we enjoyed on the way round.

As I read *The Shape of Taste* I am reminded of how Chris and his colleagues unraveled the secrets of why consumers in the north of Russia prefer their vodka in one way and why they prefer a different flavor profile in the south. They then went on to develop a flavor profile that would work in both.

This was a repeat of a process that I had also observed when Chris explained why coffee drinkers in different parts of the Philippines preferred different coffees and again developed a coffee taste profile that won preference testing in all regions.

I also remember working with Chris in Brazil identifying the best flavor profiles for an international beer company. It just so happened that we were in Brazil at the same time as the FIFA Football World Cup. No one at home would believe that it was a coincidence that we were researching beer in Brazil during the World Cup. I am not entirely sure that we believed it either.

There is no shortage of books and literature that speak about consumer emotions and emotional journeys. But I am not aware of anyone outside of The Marketing Clinic who has connected the sensory experience of consumption – the appearance, aroma, flavor, texture, even the swallow and how it feels in the stomach – to the emotional responses that these generate.

At Lindstrom Company we spend a lot of time helping big companies change the way that they manage and communicate their brands. There is no doubt in my mind when a food and beverage company understands the Shape of Taste for each of their brands. When they understand the individual features of their product that prompt the emotional journey that the product evokes in their consumers, and why, then they develop better products that improve consumers' lives, and are able to communicate them in more effective ways.

In the following pages Chris reveals some of the theory behind what he does, how we develop our own tastes, our likes and dislikes, and why – although for each of us this is an intensely personal journey – this can also be viewed at a population level.

I find it fascinating at a personal level, making me think

about how and why I respond to specific flavors and textures as I do, and at a professional level, understanding how food and beverage brands evoke emotional journeys in their consumers as a whole and how we can use this knowledge to improve those brands for our consumers and communicate them in a more accurate and empathic way.

Chris uses many great real-life examples of how this approach has been applied to brands around the world. Apart from my professional fascination with these, they also emphasized to me one of the things that I have heard Chris expound upon on a number of occasions.

Brand owners, marketers, and far too many other researchers often refer to the emotional impact of a brand as a single-dimensional, static emotion. "It makes the consumer feel energized" or "It relaxes them". It is quite apparent, however, and made very clear by *The Shape of Taste*, that anyone's emotional response to a consumption experience (in fact any experience) is a journey through a multitude of emotions. It is when we understand this journey and how and why it is prompted by the features of the consumer experience that we understand our brands and how we can best manage them.

Martin Lindstrom
Branding and culture expert, *New York Times* bestselling author
Founder and owner of Lindstrom Company

Introduction

I saw a great movie a while back and was so engrossed in the story that I had no idea how long I'd been in the movie theater. It could have been less than an hour or more than five. However, I do remember feeling somewhat disorientated when the lights came on and we all started filing out of the doors. Unusually for me, I found myself chatting with complete strangers as we picked our way down the steps towards the exit – all of us still absorbed in the story we had just witnessed, brought together, united by a shared and moving experience.

On reflection, the storyline was not profoundly different or unique. It was the way in which the story was told – the empathy that I felt for the characters; the excitement, joy, shock, and despair I felt as their stories unfolded. The cinematic experience, which had taken me on a journey with its ups and downs, twists and turns, had captivated and engaged me. It distracted me from everything else that I had to think and worry about – a brief interlude in my life that refreshed and recharged me.

This is the power of cinema, the power of great stories. However, stories are not the only things that have the power to transport you on an emotional journey. Foods can do this too.

Food and drink take you on a taste and textural journey. When that journey is well executed, then, like a great movie, it can be absorbing, distracting, and emotionally as well as physiologically refreshing and recharging.

As humans we eat and drink because we need sustenance and refreshment, but most of us are lucky enough to have a choice in what we consume and tend to choose the foods that we 'like'. Liking is an emotional reaction to an experience, so when you say you like a food or drink, what this means is that you like the way that it makes you feel.

This book is about understanding the emotional drivers behind why we like some foods and not others. It is about the taste and textural journeys that food and drink take us on and how these drive emotional journeys within us. It is about the emotional journeys of our consumption experiences.

I am a consumer psychologist and have been researching and understanding consumers' emotional responses to hundreds of products in markets all around the world for more than 20 years. I have worked for global corporations and small start-ups, researching with consumers in luxurious offices in London, Paris, and Manhattan as well as rural villages in India, shanty towns in Manila, and informal settlements across eastern and southern Africa. This book draws on much of what I have seen and experienced and distills some of the knowledge that I have collected over the years.

What this book can offer you

If you work in the food and beverage industry, this book will help you to understand why consumers respond in the way that they do to your products and to your competitors' products. It will explain why consumers respond in particular ways to your communications. It will help you to think about how you can improve your products and communicate them better. It will give you a fresh perspective through which to understand your products. It will prompt you to think about them in a completely different way.

When you understand these emotional journeys, you can create food and drinks that take consumers on great journeys and deliver real improvements in how they feel. This book explores how, as a product owner or marketer, you can use this knowledge to ensure your existing and future products deliver great emotional journeys and to improve and expand your product ranges, bringing true delight to your consumers.

If you don't work in the industry but are interested in understanding emotional responses to aromas, flavors, and textures, this book will give you an insight into why people behave and respond as they do to their food and drink. It will explain how your experiences in life shape you and determine what you like and don't like.

It may also help you to understand why you prefer the food and drinks that you like and will get you thinking about some of the foods that you avoid.

The book begins by explaining the link between the foods we eat, the beverages we drink, and our emotional responses to them. I unpick the emotional journeys that specific foods or drinks can take us on, what exactly these journeys are, how they are triggered, and why it is important to understand them in detail. I go on to establish that we make our food and beverage choices because of the way that they make us feel, that these emotional responses are rooted in our earlier life and the associative pairings that we make (more subconsciously than consciously) from a very young age.

In Chapter 2, I introduce the Shape of Taste. We developed this concept at The Marketing Clinic to show how the sensorial journey of consumption connects to – and in fact drives – the emotional journey experienced by the consumer.

Chapter 3 brings in real-life case studies to illustrate the importance of the consumer's emotional response over and above their rational response to flavor and texture. You'll find out why pursuing the 'best taste' is often a false goal as how a product makes someone feel is more important than what it actually tastes like.

Chapter 4 shows how the emotional journey – the

Shape of Taste – is what differentiates brands from their competition. Case studies sharing our work with global food and beverage brands demonstrate the importance of this journey and also how different sensorial attributes may be required to deliver ostensibly the same emotional response in different markets.

In Chapter 5, I talk about how perceptions and expectations have a significant effect on the emotional response. I look at how advertising sets up expectations for a brand and how this affects consumers' emotional response to the products. Great advertising often sets high expectations that a product may struggle to meet, undermining its ultimate success. However, you'll discover how communications that focus on a product's emotional differences against its competitors can be very powerful in building a successful brand.

Chapter 6 explores how to cope with the complexity of flavors and textures and of the emotional responses that these generate. You will find out about how the human brain deals with this complexity, what this means for taste experts such as tea and coffee tasters and for psychologists such as myself, and why understanding this complexity is crucial in understanding the Shape of Taste.

In Chapter 7, I dig a little deeper into what creates consumer trust and belief in a brand. Belief is an emotional response to a consumer's experience of a product, not a rational evaluation of its nutritional facts. Understanding the sensorial elements of the consumer's experience that prompt belief can be critical in managing ingredient changes (such as reducing fat, salt, and sugar) and in improving and innovating products.

Chapter 8 explains and gives examples of how brand owners can use the principle of the Shape of Taste to help identify opportunities for new products and to create new products and product ranges that consumers love.

Chapter 9 goes on to discuss how food cultures vary as

you move around the world and emotional responses to tastes and textures are often different in different cultures. Understanding these differences is clearly important for the owners of international brands. But equally important is understanding the similarities between different markets and how cultures are constantly evolving.

Finally, in Chapter 10, I discuss how market research results are not always what the clients want to hear when they have put months or even years into developing their products. However, once they understand the Shape of Taste and why consumers are responding as they do to their products, they are usually quick to understand how they can fix their problems.

The fascination of understanding psychology

While this book concentrates on the emotional responses to food and drink, these principles are equally applicable to any area of human experience. You will undoubtedly have noticed how people's responses, including your own, to any experience are often immediate, rarely rational, even a little inexplicable. These emotional responses spring straight out of the subconscious mind.

Often we suppress them, rationalize them, even try to deny them, but we cannot ignore them. These are learned responses and were installed into our subconscious (some psychologists call this your inner child), often in our formative years. It may just be a small part of an experience that prompts this reaction - and if you can isolate which elements prompt positive or negative responses you can start to understand yourself better.

What is really interesting is that within cultural groups, people actually share many - even quite personal - experiences, so as adults we can have the same or similar responses as our peers to a wide range of textural and flavor experiences.

Understanding the psychology of individuals is fascinating and fun for armchair psychologists. Understanding the psychology of a wide group of consumers is extremely valuable to marketers, product owners, and businesses around the world.

At The Marketing Clinic, the consultancy that I co-founded, we are food and drink psychologists and specialize in unraveling what it is that people like about certain food and beverage brands. Over the past two decades, we have worked in markets across North, South, and Central America, Asia, Europe, Africa, and Oceania, and with many of the biggest food and drink brands that you know as well as many smaller ones you may not have heard of (yet).

We help manufacturers get their tastes, textures, and aromas just right to create foods and drinks that people love. We also help them to communicate their brands in ways that entice and excite their consumers.

In this book, I would like to share some of the fascinating and often surprising things that we have learned along the way - not just about food and drink, but also about the people, cultures, and countries we have been lucky enough to meet and visit. I hope to help you understand why and how you enjoy food and drink and explain the things that unite us around the world and what it is about some of the differences that give rise to the fantastic variety of flavors, tastes, and experiences that we all love or hate as we travel between countries.

It might even help you to understand yourself a little better: why you love your favorite foods and dislike some others.

At the end of each chapter, I have inserted a few quotes in the hope that they will serve as a quick reminder of what you have read. Feel free to adapt these for your own purposes and quote them to your friends or at work. There's no need to attribute them, but they may help you to make a point or clarify a point of view.

I hope that you enjoy reading this and that you learn something valuable from it. As research is a great part of who I am, I would be very interested to hear your thoughts.

Chris Lukehurst
chris@marketingclinic.com

Chapter 1

You are what you eat

'You are what you eat,' as the saying goes. While there is truth in this, and what you put into your body certainly has a significant effect, I tend to think about it the other way around: 'You eat what you are.'

You choose your foods to suit your mood, and those choices are driven by emotions. If you are down, you may look for comfort; if you are tired, you may opt for a pick-me-up. There are certain foods and drinks that you might associate with celebration and some for commiseration. There are even drinks that do both. I am British and always look to have a cup of tea if there's been a disaster or if someone needs to talk. It's part of a cultural heritage. While the exact foods or drinks that you picture in your mind when you read these sentences may vary depending upon your culture, religion, or where you are in the world, they will also have some striking similarities.

In this chapter, you will find out about the link between the foods we eat, the beverages we drink, and our emotional responses to them. It looks at the emotional journeys that specific foods and drinks can take us on, what exactly these journeys are, how they are triggered, and why it is important to understand these journeys in detail. This chapter explores how we make our food and beverage choices because of the way that they make us feel and how these emotional responses are rooted in our earlier life and the associative pairings that we make from a very young age.

Most people – and almost certainly most who will be reading this book – are fortunate enough not to know true hunger. And if we do feel hungry or thirsty, we are frequently lucky enough to have choices in what we eat and drink. When we are in a position to make that choice – even, perhaps, between different options all of which we 'like' – we tend to select the one we 'feel like' eating or drinking today.

As if that is a proper explanation of why we made that choice!

In truth, we choose certain foods because we like the way they make us feel. Although we are rarely conscious of this, we are selecting them because we like the emotional journey they will take us on.

Before I expand upon this theme, I would like to visit a completely different area to illustrate the point.

What is your favorite movie?

You probably have a favorite movie, one that you regularly come back to late at night on your own, with your friends or partner, perhaps with family on vacation, at Christmas or other celebrations. Or maybe you have a particular music track that you always come back to when you are upset, happy, or stressed; maybe you have a favorite poem that you like to re-read or listen to...

By definition, if it is your favorite, you know it pretty well. You know the storyline, you know the twists and turns of the plot, the change in tempo part way through. You know the way that it will pick you up and take you along its path, you know the ending, and, most importantly, you know the way that you will feel at the end. There are no surprises here: You know exactly how it will change your mood. It will relax or stimulate you, it will cheer you up, or take your mind away from your problems. It will make you feel better.

You choose that movie, that music, that poem because you know how you will feel by the end.

But our moods are not that easily changed. There is not some simple switch that can be flicked to take us from stressed to relaxed, from sad to cheered. The movie, music, or poem works because it takes us on a journey. It picks us up, whatever our mood, and draws us in.

There will be some critical points in this journey – twists in the storyline, changes in tempo or key – that take our attention away from where we were and into the story. It then draws us along an emotional mood journey with highs and lows, twists and turns, and delivers us at the end exactly where we knew it would. That is why it is our favorite, because we know that we can rely on it to take us to where we want to be.

The plot, with its mood changes and surprises, will even work with a diverse group of people starting in different moods, with different thoughts, and draw them all along the same path. I mentioned in the introduction how I found myself speaking with complete strangers as I exited from a movie that had moved me. Have you ever noticed the harmony in the mood of the crowd as they leave the theater after a good movie, compared with their disparate moods and conversations at the start?

It is the same with food and drink. Over my years of research, I have consistently seen that people make their food and drink choices because they are looking for the emotional journey that choice will take them on. A consumption experience has a plot with twists and turns, highs and lows. The plot draws you in, moves you through the journey, and delivers you at the end in a different mood, a different place, than you were before you started. It even has the ability to unite a disparate group of people from different starting points, to unify their mood, bring them together, to create harmony.

So, next time you are in a filling station and you make an

impulse purchase of a bar of chocolate, stop to think about the real reason that you picked up that bar. Yes, you chose it because you saw it, and you like it, but what is the journey that your inner child was screaming at you for? This was probably not a considered rational purchase: Your subconscious – your inner child – saw that bar and screamed, "Yes, something comforting to soothe my mood. I want to be calmed down. Buy it now!" or, "That was a hard day, I need a treat. That chocolate will cheer me up, energize me…"

Eating is more than just satisfying a physiological need. Of course, we eat because we need sustenance and energy, but the real driver of our choice of food and drink is our emotions. Eating and drinking are transformational experiences that change our mood, that move us from one place to the next. As with most things in life, when we understand what our subconscious is looking for – what our inner child is seeking – we make much better, more satisfying, choices.

Each of the following chapters will use our experience at The Marketing Clinic of working with some of the biggest brands around the world to illustrate different aspects of these emotional journeys. But first I would like to turn to why eating and drinking are such emotional experiences and how emotional responses become attached to food. In other words, how our food likes and loathings are formed.

Why do you like some foods and dislike others?

As a psychologist, it is tempting to start at birth and see how our environment and experiences shape our responses to the world around us. But in this case birth is already a little late in the process.

As researchers such as Beyza Ustun and her team have shown, our first experience of taste is in the womb. The flavors of the mother's diet are transferred into the amniotic fluid and the baby in the womb picks up tastes from this fluid. So, if Mom is Mexican, the baby is likely to be exposed to hot chili flavors; if Mom is Indian, the baby will most likely be exposed to a range of spices (and if Mom is American, probably to high-fructose corn starch). So even before birth, baby is already acclimatizing to Mom's diet. This, of course, continues if baby is fed on breast milk, which again is flavored by their mother's diet, as Joanne M Spahn and other researchers have shown.

So, babies are acclimatizing to flavors in the womb and continuing to do so after they are born. But how does each of us learn to attach emotional responses to flavors and textures?

Feeding a baby is one of the most nurturing and bonding activities known to humankind. Much is said about the emotional bonding benefits of breastfeeding, but as any parent (mother and father) knows, bottle feeding is also an intimate bonding experience. As a baby experiences the strong parental love and security of being held and fed it is also experiencing the taste of the milk. This experience is consistently repeated. A baby feels loved, comforted, safe, and reassured, and it associates these positive emotional feelings with the experience of being held and hugged and with the flavors that it tastes – something that was observed by O William Anderson back in the 1950s.

The one universal taste and aroma association that I have found with my Marketing Clinic colleagues wherever we work in the world is that vanilla is always regarded as comforting and homely. It is my belief that this has its root in the vanillic flavor of mother's milk, which is in turn replicated in formula milks.

Baby is also experiencing the aromas of the parent who is feeding them and, if breastfed, the flavors of their mother's diet. While lying in their crib, baby experiences the aroma of their home, too – those familiar aromas of our own home that we do not even notice unless we have been away from it for a prolonged period or when we enter someone else's home and notice how different it smells. From a baby's very earliest days, it is acclimatizing to these tastes and aromas and pairing them with its feelings of contentment, safety, and security or with discomfort, hunger, and fear.

You may not know why you like or dislike an aroma or a taste – maybe you just always have – but the origin of that liking or dislike is probably based upon some early pairing of the flavor with positive or negative emotional experiences. And this process goes on throughout your childhood, as you associate specific tastes and textures – even different ways of delivering a taste or a texture – with the positive or negative feelings that you experienced at the same time. Psychologists call it paired associative learning.

Some foods are associated with fun and parties and will always represent carefree, exciting, fun times. Some will be associated with a parent or carer's love and home – they will always be comforting, safe, reassuring foods. Some will have less pleasant associations such as the first time you got ill through alcohol, or eating something that gave you food poisoning or made you sick, and these flavors may be challenging to you for the rest of your life.

The lasting power of celebratory foods

Cake, ice cream, and many sweet and a variety of savory dishes are encountered at celebratory events such as birthdays, weddings, and holidays. Everyone is happy, having fun, the child is getting lots of attention, and many behavior rules seem to be relaxed. Foods experienced in such a positive environment are quickly associated with the positive mood that pervades the event. In every culture, as I have myself seen time after time in my travels and research, the key celebratory foods remain widely popular with young and older age groups, as they continue to evoke the positive emotions of celebration, fun, togetherness, and happiness.

However, other foods may, often quite by accident, become associated with less pleasant emotions. Maybe you choked when eating an apple or found something unpleasant in your morning cereal. Maybe Mom or Dad pushed a little too hard when you would not eat your green beans and your young mind decided that you never did like them anyway.

And so, through your own personal experiences, you gradually build a significant collection of flavors, aromas, and textures that you associate with positive or negative emotional reactions. Most of the time you are not consciously aware of these pairings - the incident or incidents that created the pairing are long forgotten - but you do know that you like or dislike those foods.

What is really interesting from a research perspective is that although the experiences that create your lists of likes and dislikes are very personal, there are in fact huge similarities within cultures, as so many of our personal experiences are shared with - or very similar to - those of our peers.

You will probably have enjoyed the same party foods as your peers and will share the same positive associations. Your family meals, your treats, the foods that your parents or other carers pressed upon you as being good for you, and the ones that they tried to limit your consumption of, will often have shared many similarities.

Over the years, our research has shown considerable consistency, particularly of the likes, within cultural groups. It has also identified often quite significant differences between cultures, where the collective experiences of flavors and textures have been different.

The role of evolution

You may be slightly skeptical that all your preferences are learned in this way, and you may quite rightly ask about our innate likes and dislikes. You might note how young children tend to like candy and sweet things and spit out the bitter greens. Let us consider the influence of millions of years of evolution on our taste palate today.

Humans are arguably born with two innate likes and two dislikes. We like, indeed crave, sweet things and fat, as B J Cowart noted in the early 1980s. Evolutionally this was very useful, motivating us to seek out highly calorific foods to give us vital sustenance and energy. We also dislike, gag upon, and are motivated to spit out bitter and sour flavors. Again, evolutionally very useful, as most poisonous berries are bitter, while unripe fruits are sour. Our instincts trained us to seek out the foods that we needed to survive and avoid the ones that might kill us.

Those lucky enough to be born into a world of plenty are still born craving fatty and sweet foods and rejecting sour and bitter flavors, and this instinct remains throughout our early years. However, here's the fascinating bit: As we move through our teens, we learn to reject sweet and fatty flavors and learn to like bitter and sour tastes.

Exactly when this happens and the degree to which each of us will adapt our own likes and dislikes varies from individual to individual, but nearly all of us to some extent learn to move away from sweet flavors and from fat and not only endure, but in fact enjoy bitter and sour flavors.

Evolutionally, sweet and fatty foods represented survival. They were vitally important but difficult to access. Now, for many people, they are widely available, relatively easy to access, and have come to represent overindulgence, obesity, and poor health. As we grow from child to adult, we start to understand this. The more strongly we make the association between these foods and being unhealthy, the more we may start to pair the tastes and textures of sugar and fat with related negative emotions. We start to override our innate liking for these flavors and textures with a negative emotional pairing.

It is not always simple. We are accustomed to the sweetness of the foods that we like. We probably have very positive paired emotions with many of them, but these pairings are now in contrast to a more conscious concern over the effects of consuming too much sugar or fat.

You may yourself remember making a conscious effort to reduce your sugar or fat intake. Perhaps, to give an example, you decided to give up sugar in tea. At first it tastes awful – "How can anyone get used to drinking it like this?" – but you are determined to reduce your sugar intake, so you persevere. After a while, you stop noticing how awful it tastes and get used to drinking it without sugar. Six months later your mom, gran, or a friend, who has forgotten that you have given up sugar, passes you a cup with sugar, how you used to drink it. It is disgusting, and you can't believe that you used to enjoy tea like this.

It is around the same time in life that we also teach ourselves to like sour and bitter flavors.

As a child, there was no need to like bitter or sour foods. You may have been encouraged to eat greens or broccoli, but you could usually get away with throwing them across the room (or feeding them to the dog as you got a little older and the temper tantrums didn't seem to work so well). But you did observe that there were some foods and drinks the adults seemed to enjoy, but when you and your friends or siblings tried them, you found them unpalatable.

Coffee, olives, alcoholic drinks... they were grown-ups' foods that were part of being an adult but not relevant to you as a child. Then you became a teenager and, to identify with the adults, you wanted to eat and drink grown-up foods. So now you try them again...

But hang on a minute... they haven't got any better, they still taste disgusting.

However, you are an adult now and you must be seen to be one, both by your parents and by your friends. You don't admit it tastes awful because that would be childish, and that you definitely are not. Besides, all your friends are enjoying their coffee/beer so you are not going to be the odd one out (they, of course, are struggling with it as much as you are, but they are not going to admit that either).

What is important here is that, apart from the taste of the drink, you are enjoying the sociability of the occasion, sitting drinking together like real adults, and you rather like the way the drink makes you feel. You persevere. You are happy to repeat the event. It was fun, grown-up, and made you feel good. Each time it is a little easier to swallow the drink. Soon you find that it does not distract from the occasion at all, and then that you are actually enjoying the drink as well as the occasion. Another example of associative learning, the principle of evolving our tastes through the experience of external stimuli is well established in psychology (De Houwer, Thomas and Baeye 2001).

By pairing the flavor with positive emotions such as feeling adult, acquiring a more sophisticated palate, and being at fun, sociable events, you overcome your innate dislike for the bitter flavor and quickly find that you rather like it. You have acquired the taste for it.

So even innate likes and dislikes that evolved over millions of years can be changed in a matter of months. Eating is a sensory journey but our enjoyment or otherwise of that sensory journey is emotional. It is founded in those associative pairings that we make in the early years of our lives and the adaptations we make as we develop and grow.

What can we learn from Alfred Hitchcock?
Let's go back to the movies for a moment...

Alfred Hitchcock was known as the master of suspense and was famous for the way he framed his shots to maximize anxiety, fear, and empathy. Hitchcock absolutely understood that he was taking his viewers on an emotional journey. In fact, this was so important to him that he always had two scripts.

The 'blue script' included the actors' lines, the stage directions, lighting directions, and sound. It encompassed everything that was actually happening on screen, frame by frame. But what many people don't know is that Hitchcock also had a 'green script'. This outlined the emotional response he wanted his audience to feel at each moment of the movie. It detailed when he wanted them to be calm and relaxed, when the suspense should build, and when it would drop away – and when he was going to scare the living daylights out of them.

By having both the green script and the blue script, Hitchcock crafted a unique and memorable emotional journey for his viewers and thus remarkable movies that have outlived the man himself.

Most food manufacturers and marketers have their blue script. They know all the stage directions, they know their lines, what must be done, and how to do it. But few have a comprehensive green script describing the optimum emotional journey they should be orchestrating for their consumer – how they can execute skillful twists and turns in that journey, highs and lows to create a memorable, evocative, and fulfilling journey that consumers enjoy and are keen to repeat again and again.

Hitchcock started with the emotional journey that he wanted his viewers to experience and then made his movie to deliver that experience. His green script was his map; the blue script was simply the way to deliver it.

At The Marketing Clinic, we help food and drink manufacturers to identify and understand their green script so they can focus their energies on delivering the best emotional journeys for their consumers.

Key ideas from this chapter

🍴 You eat what you are – you choose your foods to suit your mood, and those choices are driven by emotions.

🍴 We choose certain foods because we like the way they make us feel. We like the emotional journey they will take us on.

🍴 A consumption experience is an emotional journey. It has a plot: The journey has its twists and turns, its highs and its lows. The plot draws you in, moves you through the journey, and delivers you at the end in a different mood, a different place than you were before you started.

🍴 Through your own personal experiences, you gradually build a significant collection of flavors, aromas, and textures that you associate with positive or negative emotional reactions. Most of the time you are not consciously aware of these pairings – the incident or incidents that created the pairing are long forgotten – but you do know that you like or dislike those foods.

🍴 Although the experiences that create your lists of likes and dislikes are very personal, there are in fact huge similarities within cultures as so many of our personal experiences are shared with, or very similar to, those of our peers.

🍴 Alfred Hitchcock started with the emotional journey that he wanted his viewers to experience and then made his movie to deliver that experience. His green script was his map, the blue script simply the way to deliver it.

Chapter 2

The Shape of Taste

Chapter 1 discussed how every consumption experience changes your mood and that it does this by taking you on a sensorial and emotional journey. If you are to understand how and why people react in particular ways to their food and beverages, you need to understand these journeys. In this chapter, I introduce the concept of the Shape of Taste, showing how the sensorial journey of consumption connects to, and in fact drives, the emotional journey experienced by the consumer.

Like any other journey, and like a good movie, each consumption journey has a start point, a number of twists and turns, maybe a few waypoints en route, and then it has an endpoint. It is a physiological journey and a psychological one.

It is relatively simple to track that physiological (taste and textural) journey, to understand its twists and turns, its waypoints, the levels of sweetness, sourness, and bitterness. The initial taste hit, the rear-of-mouth experience, the aftertaste. You can submit this to all sorts of detailed analyses and show how different flavors, levels of sweetness, textures, and other aspects affect liking, preference, and repeat purchase. But while such a detailed map of the physiological journey may make you better informed, does it make you any wiser? Does it improve your useful knowledge or help your decision making?

A Milky Way (or a Mars Bar as it is called outside the US) starts with the crack of the outer chocolate, then the softness of the interior. The release of the aroma of the caramel and nougat, the contrasting consistencies as the hard outside chocolate, the softer nougat, and the almost liquid caramel are chewed together. The harmony as the three elements merge together and melt away. The clear from the mouth, the aftertaste... and then the second bite.

However, as any travel writer will tell you, the route itself is not the important part of the journey. It simply connects points on a map. It is data, it informs us, tells us what is happening, but does not answer the important questions:

- So what?
- Why?
- What do we do about it?

It's all about the emotions

What makes the journey enjoyable (or otherwise) are the emotions that it provokes – the traveler's emotional reactions to the journey, to its twists and turns, to the waypoints, to the scenery observed as they pass by. Travel books make a great read not because you experience the journey (because you don't, sitting at home reading the book) but because they share the emotions of the traveler. The writer communicates their emotional reactions to what they see and experience and evokes an emotional reaction in you through their descriptions and the stories that they tell. It is because you experience the emotions that you feel you are on the journey with the writer.

It's possible to track the emotional journey of the consumer as they eat their chocolate bar. What is the consumer's emotional reaction to the crack of the chocolate and the bite into the softer caramel and nougat? How do they respond to the aroma that is released as they break the chocolate coating? To the mix of textures as they chew the bar and to the merging and the melt of the different elements?

Now you have a much more interesting tale. Now you can see the consumer's physiological journey – their route – and you can see their emotional journey, their reaction to their experience of that route.

Understanding the whole emotional journey, not just the endpoint

You may think that marketers and advertisers have been using the emotions associated with products since the start of last century. There is nothing new in using consumers' emotional responses to products to make great advertising that appeals at an emotional level. But the real trick is to understand exactly which features of the physiological sensory journey prompt which emotional reactions. How do the individual elements of the journey build up to create the final emotional response and why do these elements have that overall emotional effect?

It is also helpful if you understand what makes a good emotional journey. How does the journey build up? It will have its highs and its lows, but how should these interact to produce the best consumer experience? Are there elements of the journey that are, by definition, negative or positive, or, with the right juxtaposition, do certain 'negative' emotions emphasize the positive and improve the consumer's overall reaction?

In our experience at The Marketing Clinic, we have often found that brand owners over-focus on and have an oversimplified view of the positive elements. They ignore the sequencing, intensity, and nature of the whole emotional journey, which may deliver an overarching positive effect that is emphasized and thus enhanced by the occasional 'negative' aspect.

This is quite a leap. Many brand owners think they

understand the emotions associated with their products. But do they really understand which elements of their product prompt which emotional responses and why?

They may know how consumers respond to their products, but do they know what a 'better' response might look like, and how to make a product to evoke that better response?

This is where we can learn from Alfred Hitchcock and his use of the blue and green scripts. As you read in Chapter 1, Hitchcock's green script was his map, the blue script simply the way to deliver it.

Brand owners too need to understand their green script first and then focus their energies on how they deliver the best emotional journeys for their consumers.

Great things rarely happen by accident

When I attended the wedding of some close friends, we all filed out after the ceremony into the gardens for the traditional photographs and confetti throwing. The photographer then escorted the happy couple for a walk to the nearby venue where the next stage of the celebrations would continue. However, he did not take them directly to their destination.

Unbeknown to them, he had checked out an alternative route. While apparently casually chatting away and snapping a few informal additional shots, he led them past spectacular backdrops, framed superb pictures, and caught them unawares every time. The couple had no idea what was happening until they saw the pictures, which were breathtaking.

It did not happen by accident. The photographer knew exactly what he wanted to achieve; he then scouted out and devised the route. He knew how he wanted to frame each shot, knew where he had to be positioned as they walked into each frame, even where he needed to direct their attention and when. He knew exactly what he wanted to achieve first – he had his green script – and then he set out a plan to achieve his blue script.

Why the Shape of Taste is so important

At The Marketing Clinic we have developed the Shape of Taste as a way to illustrate this when dealing with food and drink. The Shape of Taste charts the consumption journey of any food or drink. It describes the sensorial experience of the consumer and demonstrates how this evokes a corresponding emotional journey. Once you start to think about your consumption experiences as a Shape of Taste, you start to think about everything you consume differently, and if you happen to be the brand owner responsible for the product development or communication of a food or drink product, it helps you to think differently about what you do.

Some examples can help to convey what I mean by the Shape of Taste and why it is so crucial to understand and work with it.

Over the years, The Marketing Clinic has accumulated huge amounts of experience working on coffee - coffee grounds and instant coffee, coffee shop coffee, machine-dispensed coffee, coffee in the office, out of home, at home, in markets from the US and Europe to Brazil, Mexico, Thailand, China, and the Philippines.

Coffee is a fascinating product to research because in nearly all markets it awakens and stimulates as well as calms and relaxes. Understanding how one product can do both things and understanding how to manage and communicate the sensorial journey in order to optimize the emotional one is challenging and very rewarding.

Exactly how coffee achieves its magical trick does vary in different markets. Consumers in markets where there is a strong coffee tradition receive different messages from their coffee than those in markets where the tradition is generally tea based. In areas where coffee beans are grown, attitudes are shaped by the availability of the coffee, how it has traditionally been prepared, and, of course, by the type of local beans.

There is never just a simple answer: "This is the best coffee." First, you need to understand the specific emotional journey the local consumer is seeking, and then you need to establish the best way to deliver that journey for them in that environment.

On the following pages are three Shapes of Taste, showing three very different types of coffee journey and how they are delivered. These are simplified and without the more detailed explanations of why and how, but they will give you an insight into how, once you understand the emotional journey required, you can prompt that journey through your sensorial delivery.

The charts use **bold** text for the sensorial journey (above the curve) and *italics* for the emotional journey (below).

If you drink coffee, as you look at these, think about your own favorite coffee (in fact, why not make yourself one before you carry on reading?). Do you like an immediate intensity or an easier start to your sip? Do you like a growing bitterness or a smoother, gentler experience? A strong aftertaste or a milder finish?

Then think about how your coffee makes you feel.

As you follow the curves of the Shape of Taste for each coffee in the graphs, imagine the taste of that coffee in your mouth. Think about your emotional response to that feeling. You may even start to re-evaluate what you like about coffee and think about the brands that you buy.

Coffee 1 has a smooth, silky start; it tastes slightly sweet with a just hint of sharpness. The drinker is not immediately assaulted with a strong hit. They can ease into this coffee. The bitterness then builds throughout the mouth. A complexity and depth of flavor become apparent. This is stimulating and awakening; it feels like a sophisticated adult drink.

After a fast build in bitterness and complexity, the flavor plateaus as the drink moves into the rear of the mouth. It does not become too intense. The consumer has time to appreciate the depth and complexity.

Shape of Taste: Coffee 1

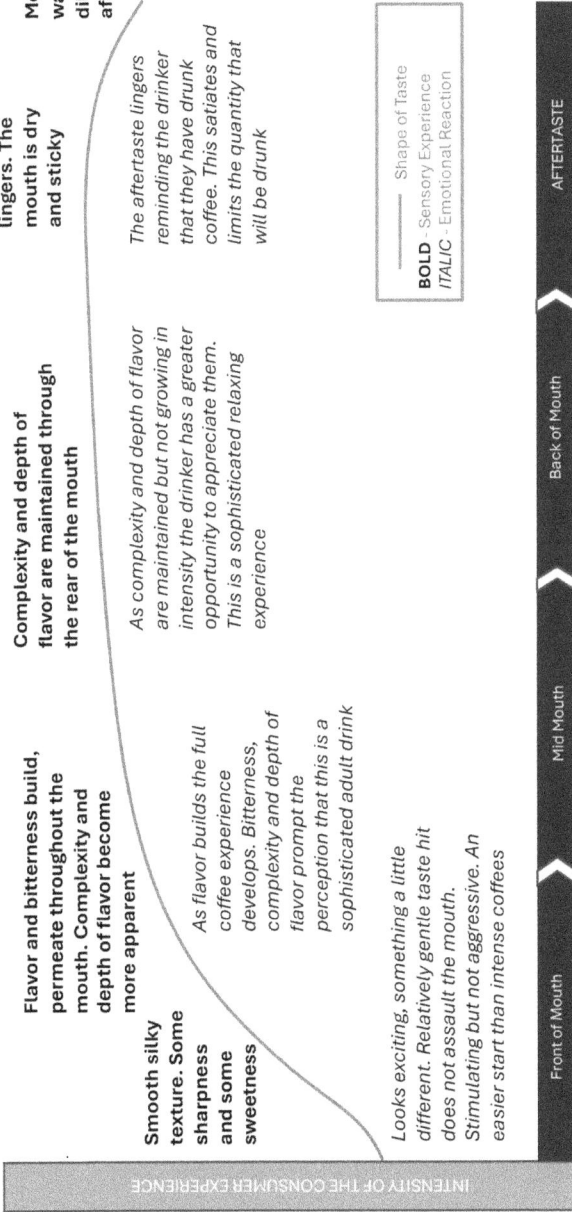

Smooth silky texture. Some sharpness and some sweetness

Looks exciting, something a little different. Relatively gentle taste hit does not assault the mouth. Stimulating but not aggressive. An easier start than intense coffees

Flavor and bitterness build, permeate throughout the mouth. Complexity and depth of flavor become more apparent

As flavor builds the full coffee experience develops. Bitterness, complexity and depth of flavor prompt the perception that this is a sophisticated adult drink

Complexity and depth of flavor are maintained through the rear of the mouth

As complexity and depth of flavor are maintained but not growing in intensity the drinker has a greater opportunity to appreciate them. This is a sophisticated relaxing experience

Aftertaste lingers. The mouth is dry and sticky

The aftertaste lingers reminding the drinker that they have drunk coffee. This satiates and limits the quantity that will be drunk

Mouth waters and dilutes aftertaste

——— Shape of Taste
BOLD - Sensory Experience
ITALIC - Emotional Reaction

| Front of Mouth | Mid Mouth | Back of Mouth | AFTERTASTE |

INTENSITY OF THE CONSUMER EXPERIENCE

Shape of Taste: Coffee 2

Shape of Taste
BOLD - Sensory Experience
ITALIC - Emotional Reaction

Smooth, silky, a little acidic. Thin watery and a little sweet.

A very gentle introduction does not demand attention or stimulate the drinker

Flavor, bitterness and complexity gently build

As bitterness and complexity build the drinker is calmed and relaxed. This coffee can be appreciated without effort

The mouth is filled with a light but rich complexity of flavor with bitterness complemented by sweeter notes

Lightness of flavor and complexity remain at the tear of the mouth, but the coffee is a little watery

Watery lighter flavor at the back of the mouth is refreshing and unchallenging

Aftertaste is brief, a little drying. Mouth waters

Brief watery aftertaste leaves the drinker remembering and wanting to repeat the calming complexity of the mid-mouth taste. The lack of much aftertaste means the coffee is not satiating

Front of Mouth   Mid Mouth   Back of Mouth   AFTERTASTE

INTENSITY OF THE CONSUMER EXPERIENCE

28

Shape of Taste: Coffee 3

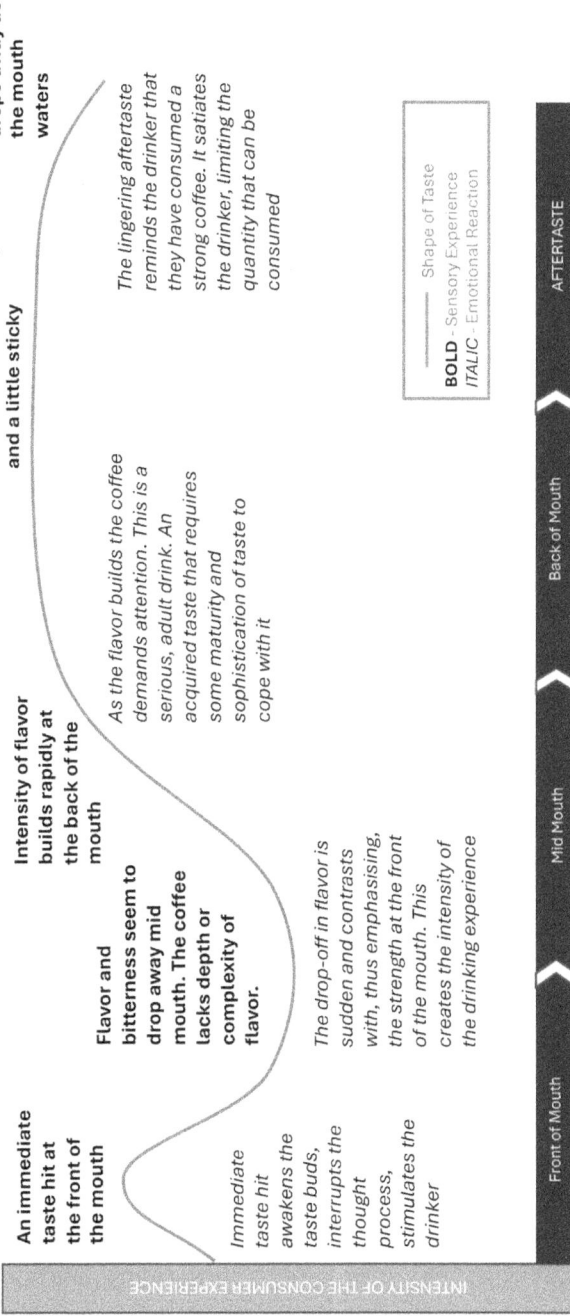

An immediate taste hit at the front of the mouth

Immediate taste hit awakens the taste buds, interrupts the thought process, stimulates the drinker

Flavor and bitterness seem to drop away mid mouth. The coffee lacks depth or complexity of flavor.

The drop-off in flavor is sudden and contrasts with, thus emphasising, the strength at the front of the mouth. This creates the intensity of the drinking experience

Intensity of flavor builds rapidly at the back of the mouth

As the flavor builds the coffee demands attention. This is a serious, adult drink. An acquired taste that requires some maturity and sophistication of taste to cope with it

Aftertaste lingers at the back of the mouth and in the throat. Mouth is dry and a little sticky

The lingering aftertaste reminds the drinker that they have consumed a strong coffee. It satiates the drinker, limiting the quantity that can be consumed

Aftertaste is diluted and drops away as the mouth waters

Shape of Taste
BOLD - Sensory Experience
ITALIC - Emotional Reaction

Front of Mouth | Mid Mouth | Back of Mouth | AFTERTASTE

INTENSITY OF THE CONSUMER EXPERIENCE

29

The aftertaste lingers in the mouth at a similar intensity. The mouth feels dry and a little sticky. The drinker is very aware they have drunk a strong coffee. They will feel stimulated and awakened. The lingering aftertaste causes the drinker to feel satisfied, sated, and limits the quantity that will be drunk.

Coffee 2 starts smooth and silky. It is slightly acidic; it feels a little thin and watery, a little sweet. This is a very gentle, easy start. It does not demand the drinker's attention, nor does it stimulate the drinker.

There is a slight build in bitterness and complexity. The mouth is filled with a subtle, rich complexity of flavor. A slight bitter edge is complemented by sweeter notes. This is a calming, easy coffee that can be appreciated without effort. The aftertaste is brief; it fades quickly. The drinker is left seeking another mouthful for its relaxed, subtle complexity. This coffee is not particularly awakening or stimulating.

Coffee 3 has an immediate taste hit that demands the drinker's attention. Straight away, it is awakening and stimulating. The flavor and bitterness then seem to drop away. The drinker briefly relaxes. The strength and bitterness do not become overwhelming. The intensity of flavor then increases again as the drink moves into the rear of the mouth. It reaches a greater intensity, demanding more attention. This is very awakening and stimulating.

The mouth waters and, as the drink is swallowed, this dilutes its strength, moderating the impression of intensity. The drinker is stimulated and awoken but also starts to relax. The brief interlude of intensity in the mid mouth gives this drink more character, preventing it from becoming overwhelming, while also serving to emphasize its strength.

As you can see, the Shape of Taste connects the sensorial qualities of a food or beverage to the emotional responses that it evokes in the consumer. Looking at this journey, you can identify a series of individual moments in the consumption experience that prompt emotional responses. But, as in any journey, it is not just the individual moments that matter; it is also their relative intensity and sequencing that have a significant effect on the consumer's overall reaction.

Every Shape of Taste is unique

I am a cyclist. As any cyclist knows, the journey is not just about getting from A to B. It is really about all the points in between. It is not just about how many meters you climb, but also about how steep the climbs are and the gaps (rests) between each ascent. It is about how sudden and how sharp the corners are and also whether the sharpest corners are on the flat or on the fast descents. It is about the sequencing of these features on the journey. Are all the big climbs in the first half of the ride while you are still fresh? Or does this route save the biggest and steepest climb for just before the finish?

This is also true of taste journeys. A flat, unchanging, uniform experience is simple, unchallenging but boring and unexciting. Something that starts with an intense taste straight away may be exciting – probably quite moreish – but is likely to feel artificial and ultimately lack satisfaction. Your reaction to any bitterness in a flavor is invariably dependent upon how suddenly that bitterness occurs – how steep the climb is to its peak. More importantly, if bitterness is preceded by some sweetness, the reaction to the bitter flavor will be exaggerated, while if the sweetness comes afterward, you will find the intensity of the bitterness much more bearable.

Every Shape of Taste is unique, with different sequences and intensities of flavors, with different gradients, different twists and turns along the way. It is these 'features' (moments) in the journey, just as much as the different tastes and textures themselves, that evoke the consumer's emotional response. When you understand all these characteristics of the journey and how and why they evoke the emotional responses that they do, you will understand your foods and drinks better.

You will learn to appreciate their subtleties more fully. You may also start to understand more about yourself.

If you work in the food and drink industry, you will find that you are in a position to adapt the taste journeys of your products to deliver more satisfying emotional journeys to your consumers.

Even better, when you can identify the ideal Shape of Taste that your consumers are looking for, you can then create a product to deliver a taste journey that will evoke the desired emotional outcome.

Testing out taste journeys for yourself

Why not try it for yourself? Pick a drink, a piece of confectionery, or a snack item that you eat or drink regularly.

Look at it and think about how that makes you feel. Are you excited? Does it make you want to consume it? Are you bored, untouched by its appearance? Ask yourself why you feel this way.

Smell it. Does it remind you of anything? Does it prompt any memories? Does the aroma fit with the appearance? How does it make you feel?

Take a bite or a sip. What is your immediate impression? Does this fit with the appearance and the aroma? Does it deliver upon the promise of the aroma? Is it better or not as good as expected? How do you feel as you get this first impression? Do you feel differently from how you did before?

As you chew it, or move the liquid back through your mouth, how do the flavor and texture change? Does the flavor grow or decline? Does it become sweeter or less sweet? Does your mouth water? Is your experience getting better or is this not as good as the initial taste? Where does your attention focus? Is it on the flavor or on the texture? Does the product melt and fill your mouth with flavor? Does it pass through your mouth quickly or slowly? How do you feel now?

At the back of your mouth, just before and as you swallow,

how does it feel now? How has the flavor changed, what can you taste? Do you feel yourself relaxing, slowing down, or are you stimulated and speeding up?

Is there an aftertaste? Is there more taste after swallowing than there was while it was in your mouth? Is the aftertaste different from when it was in your mouth? What can you taste? How do you feel now?

Has the product delivered on your expectations? Has it delivered on the promise of its appearance and aroma? Does it deliver on the promise of its advertising?

Think about the sensorial journey that you have just experienced. Think about the emotional journey, about how each stage made you feel, about how your thoughts, your focus, your feelings moved as you ate or drank it.

Maybe you find this easy to do or maybe you find it a little challenging. But give it some time. Try it with a few different products. You may find that you start to think a little differently about some of the foods that you eat and about how they make you feel. You may find that you change some of the foods you choose as you give them a little more thought while you eat them. You may start to realize why you like certain foods and drinks and not others, or why you prefer this particular brand to another. You might even find yourself setting off on a nostalgic journey into your childhood prompted by an aroma, a taste, a texture, or a particular sequence of these that you have not given much thought to for a while.

Understanding how and why you respond to certain aromas, tastes, and textures can be enlightening as to why you make some of the choices that you do and why you feel as you do about certain foods and drinks.

Before you did this exercise, you may have said that you prefer a chosen brand because it is more or less salty, sweeter or less sweet, or perhaps you preferred this flavor. Now, however, maybe you can explain to yourself (and even to other people) why it is that you prefer those sensorial differences –

the emotions that they evoke, how they make you feel.

Now you can understand why the mint version just does not work as well for you as the strawberry and, perhaps, you will also be able to suggest that if the mint flavor was delivered in a slightly different way - a smoother, less aggressive mint, slightly later in the mouth - it might have improved it for you.

Key ideas from this chapter

🍴 It's all about the emotions.

🍴 Many brand owners think they understand the emotions associated with their products. But do they really understand which elements of their product prompt what emotional responses and why?

🍴 The Shape of Taste charts the consumption journey of any food or drink. It describes the sensorial experience of the consumer and demonstrates how this evokes a corresponding emotional journey.

🍴 When you understand all the ups and downs, twists and turns of the journey, and how and why they evoke the emotional responses that they do, you will understand your foods and drinks better. You will learn to appreciate their subtleties more fully. You may also start to understand more about yourself.

Chapter 3

It's not about the best taste... it's about how it makes you feel

In Chapters 1 and 2, I talked about the connections between the sensorial experience of consumption and the consumer's emotional reaction, and introduced the Shape of Taste as a way of showing and understanding this connection. In this chapter I will share with you some real-world case studies from my research around the globe so you can see how this understanding can be used.

One thing these case studies show is that the best products are not those that taste best but the ones that evoke the best emotional responses. In Chapter 4, I will go on to show that it is this emotional journey that is the essence of the brand.

Learning from potato chips in the UK

Lay's is the dominant potato chip brand in most markets around the world. If you live in the UK, you will call them crisps rather than potato chips and know the brand as Walkers, or it's Smiths if you are in Australia, Sabritas in Mexico, or Tapuchips in Israel.

In the UK, Walkers faces heavy competition in the premium crisp market from brands such as Tyrrell's and Kettle Chips as well as the supermarket own brands, all vying for market share. In the mass market, everyday crisps (potato chips) sector, Walkers has very little branded competition, but faces increasingly strong rivalry from the supermarket own brands. These everyday chips are invariably bought to eat alongside a sandwich at lunchtime or as a quick snack between meals. They are a staple part of many children's and adults' lunch boxes.

Walkers offers a wide variety of flavors and is constantly introducing exciting new and different options. But 80 percent of sales come from five core flavors: ready salted, cheese and onion, salt and vinegar, roast chicken, and prawn cocktail.

These are long-established flavors in the UK market (although roast chicken and prawn cocktail are slightly later additions) and are immensely popular. It is these flavors that the supermarkets target with their own-label versions. In recent years the own-label potato chips had successfully closed the gap between their flavors and the Walkers versions. Increasingly, we were told in our brief from the client, consumers were saying that the own-label potato chips were "nearly as good" as Walkers and that their children especially "did not notice the difference." They were questioning whether it was worth paying the small premium for Walkers over the supermarket own brands.

Walkers' dominant share was being eroded.

The obvious answer to gain market share would be to improve the Walkers flavors. This would not be too difficult, as none of these potato chips really taste like their flavor description. With modern flavor technologies it would be quite easy to qualitatively improve these flavors, to bring them significantly closer to the flavors that their names suggest. In fact, with the possible exception of prawn cocktail, there were multiple other chips, mostly in the more premium sector that tasted much closer to these flavor descriptions. But none of these 'better' versions were anywhere near as popular as the current chips. Whenever Walkers did try to 'improve' its flavors, it received a flood of consumer complaints asking why they were changing such an iconic flavor.

These are flavors that British consumers have grown up with. They are the flavors that they love. It may not be a genuine cheese and onion flavor, but it is the flavor of cheese and onion potato chips, and that is what consumers are wanting and expecting when they choose to buy these.

The key to improving the Walkers taste journey

It was at this point that the team at Walkers asked us to get involved. They understood that people loved their flavors as they were, but they also knew that increasing numbers of consumers were buying the own-label potato chips as they were "nearly as good" anyway. How could they 'improve' Walkers' flavors to reopen the gap between themselves and the own-label competition while still retaining the important elements of the current 'imperfect' flavors that their consumers loved?

It was obvious to us, as I am sure it is to you by now, that the 'best' flavor was not about being the nearest to the flavor description, but about producing a flavor – in fact, a whole consumption experience – that evoked the right set of emotions in the consumer.

We started by understanding the emotional journey that these chips evoked. This was not simply how well the different flavors worked with a lunchtime sandwich or how they created a great snack for a mid-morning or afternoon break. It was about the conscious and unconscious emotions that the chips evoked in the consumer – how these flavors and textures were part of their childhood and teenage years, how they had grown up with them, how they cued feelings of familiarity, safety, and security. How they reminded consumers of fun, relaxed, easier times of their life. How they calmed and reassured them.

This was not just about how consumers felt after they had finished the pack. There were tiny elements of the taste and textural experience that prompted fleeting, often unconscious emotional reactions. As when you ride on a rollercoaster, it's not that you traveled from the start to the endpoint that makes you feel so exhilarated (or terrified and sick) as you dismount. It's the ups and downs, the sudden twists and turns of the journey, many of which you may not be able to precisely recall afterward, that create that feeling.

In my experience of working with with The Marketing Clinic, most consumers cannot articulate why, but they know they feel better after eating the potato chips. They tell us that they love that flavor, but what they mean is that they love the way that flavor makes them feel.

Once we understood this emotional journey, we understood what was important about these flavors. We understood how the flavors and textures prompted the emotional journey, what the important elements were, and how they worked together in creating the important emotions. In this way, we understood what we could and what we could not change if our consumers were to continue to love these flavors.

We understood the strengths and weaknesses of the Walkers potato chips and also those of its competitors and identified how we could update the Walkers flavors in a way that retained this important emotional journey, but also introduced another more contemporary, important emotion. An emotion that was not present in the competitors' chips and was also in sync with the Walkers brand positioning.

We showed the flavor development team how this new element could be incorporated into their flavors without derailing the current consumer emotional journey and how and why this added to, rather than distracted from, the consumer experience.

I recall that during the discussions of our findings and recommendations the team challenged us: "So, if this change is so subtle that many consumers will not even consciously notice it, how will it improve our performance against the own brands?" But The Marketing Clinic's work demonstrated how even a very subtle change of flavor can make a significant difference to the consumers' emotional response. We also showed how the changes we were suggesting maintained all the important old emotions and added a modernizing update – one that would differentiate these chips from their competition.

The team set to work and updated the Walkers core flavors. As soon as they started testing them, the client was so pleased with our work that we were asked to do the same thing for the core flavors in its biggest, most important market: the US.

The core flavors in the US are different – BBQ and sour cream and onion. The competitive issues are also different, even the emotional journeys, but the underlying question was the same: "How do we update the most popular flavors we have to move further ahead of the competition?"

Focus on the emotions

The Walkers example shows so well that when companies are developing food or drink products the pursuit of the 'best taste' is a false, even an ethereal, goal. In this case, achieving a qualitatively better taste would have been relatively simple but had already been shown not to work. More commonly, defining the 'best' taste is the problem, as there are as many different opinions about what this might be as the number of people that you ask.

What manufacturers need to achieve is a product that makes the consumer feel good. Aroma, taste, and texture should be seen as tools they can use to create the desired emotional response from their consumers.

It is the same if you are cooking a meal for your partner, your family, your friends. You strive to get the flavor just right. You want them to enjoy the meal you are preparing. But there will be as many opinions about exactly how hot the chili should be, or how much salt is exactly right, as there will be people eating the meal. As long as you fall within reasonable margins of acceptability, your guests will enjoy the meal because of how it makes them feel, rather than because you added or withheld that extra pinch of spice.

Think back through your lifetime of memories to the one meal that stands out as your favorite – the meal that you would love to recreate, that you go back to in your head with a feeling of nostalgia. The memory may bring you great joy, maybe a little sadness, but it is probably one of your fondest, most cherished memories. You remember the food, but also the location, even more importantly, the company, the occasion. You remember how you felt.

Now be brutally honest. Was it the best food that you have ever eaten?

The answer, for the vast majority of people, is that it was not the best food they have had. Perhaps the food did taste great, but it was the intensity of your emotions, the way that you felt that made that meal such a great memory. It was the people, the occasion, the feeling.

You may think this is a little unfair – it was the occasion that was special, not the meal. So, a slightly different question: What is your favorite meal?

It is probably not a Michelin-starred offering from the best restaurant in the country. It is far more likely to be something that your gran cooks especially for you, or your mom's Sunday lunch, your partner's special curry, your favorite takeout from that great place around the corner, or even any meal that someone else cooks for you for a change.

Undoubtedly all these meals have their merits. But they are not your favorite because they are objectively the best-tasting meals that you have ever eaten. They are special to you because of the way they make you feel. Your gran's cooking is a representation of the special relationship that you have. It reminds you of all the special moments that you have shared. It reaffirms your bond. The smell of the cooking, the taste of the meal, reassure you, make you feel safe and loved. They remind you of your gran.

Mom's Sunday lunch is family. Nothing feels quite the same as sitting down to the weekly family meal. It is about the love and caring of family and your shared history, good and not so great. It is about belonging. There are individual elements to this meal that no one does quite like Mom. It is the way they all come together on the plate, maybe even some elements to the way that it is served. No one cooks Sunday lunch like Mom – some may cook it better, but it still does not feel the same.

Your partner's special curry may taste delicious, or it may be quite mediocre, but it is always cooked with love. It was the first meal that they ever cooked for you; it is part of your shared history, a quiet night in together.

We love these meals. Their meaning goes far beyond the way that the ingredients have been prepared and cooked. They taste good, yes, but what makes them great is what that taste represents to us. We humans are sensual beings. Aromas, flavors, and textures evoke strong emotions within us. It is these emotions that cause us to like or dislike food, drink and, in fact, almost anything that we experience.

A non-food example – because it is the emotions that matter

While this book is primarily about the emotional journeys of food and drink, I thought I would include this example to demonstrate that any experience prompts an emotional journey and it is the journey that the recipient of that experience tends to evaluate rather than the experience itself.

Voltaren (Voltarol in the UK) is the number one topical pain reliever worldwide. It is a gel or cream that you rub onto aching muscles and joints to relieve discomfort. Its effectiveness is clinically proven, meaning that GSK (now Haleon), who owns the brand, has done clinical tests to prove this. It actually does what it says on the tube.

You might expect this to be the case for all 'pain-relieving' gels and creams. It is, in fact, not so. Many products in this category are not clinically proven to be effective, yet many people regularly use them to relieve aches and pains. They believe these products to be totally effective and insist on their effectiveness to their friends, families, and colleagues.

Most people are not judging the creams in the same way as the scientists who prove their clinical efficacy. They are judging based on how the cream or gel makes them feel.

When someone has an ache or a pain, when they feel restricted in what they want to do, they want a cream that will relieve the pain and allow them to just get on with life. They want to rub the cream into the affected area and then forget about it and move on.

Any truly effective analgesic or anti-inflammatory ingredient will take some time – even a few days of regular use – to work, but users formulate their opinion about the effectiveness of the cream either while they rub it in or within seconds of having done so. Maybe it warms or cools the affected area, maybe they associate the smell of it with effectiveness. Whatever it is they take their prompts from, it is the sensory experience of its use that makes them believe in this cream, long before it has any chance of actually being effective (that sensory experience also underpins any element of the placebo effect).

By understanding this sensory journey and the emotions that it evokes when consumers use the cream, we could recommend to the Voltaren team a sensory journey that, while still distinctive from their competitors and very much in keeping with their brand, would prompt a much greater belief in the effectiveness of their cream.

I hope that now you can see that while flavor is really important it is not the end in itself. What is important is the whole emotional journey that the consumption experience takes the consumer on. It is this journey that evokes liking or otherwise.

In Chapter 4, I build on this idea and show that it is this journey - the Shape of Taste - that is the essence of the brand. It is this journey that differentiates a brand from its competitors and that prompts consumers to prefer one brand over another.

Key ideas from this chapter

🍴 The best products are not those that taste best but the ones that evoke the best emotional responses.

🍴 Pursuit of the 'best taste' is a false, even an ethereal goal.

🍴 Consumers tell us that they love that flavor, but what they mean is they love the way that flavor makes them feel.

🍴 Having the 'best' flavor is not about a qualitatively better flavor, but about producing a flavor – in fact, a whole consumption experience – that evokes the right set of emotions in the consumer.

🍴 Aroma, taste, and texture should be seen as tools you can use to create the desired emotional response from your consumers.

Chapter 4

It's the journey that is the essence of the brand

As we've seen, it's the whole journey that is important, not just the endpoint. Every brand owner and marketer that I speak with enthusiastically tells me about how their product makes people feel, but they are nearly always talking about the endpoint, the end of the journey. All too rarely have they any understanding of the journey itself, of how and why their product moved the consumer to the way they feel at the finish.

Often the endpoint is a category benefit – all sodas are refreshing. It is the journey to the endpoint that differentiates a brand from its competitors. Following on from Chapter 3, this chapter explores that journey further, showing how it can bring crucial insights, which you will see from examples of our work with global brands as they sought success in different territories.

In the previous chapter, while talking about Walkers potato chips (see pages 37 to 41), I mentioned a rollercoaster. I often talk about the experience of a rollercoaster when explaining the importance of the whole journey.

Imagine yourself at a fairground, waiting for a rollercoaster ride. When you climb into the car you are not thinking about your destination. In fact, your destination is probably a matter of feet from where you are when you begin, and it looks very much like your current position. But when you get out of your seat and disembark, you will probably be feeling very differently from how you feel right now, before your ride.

Were I, or anyone else, to interview you as you climb out of the car onto the firmer ground of the platform, we would be likely to observe that you are in a heightened emotional state. You may be quite excited, exhilarated, or maybe you are feeling frightened, even a little sick – maybe all of these at the same time.

If I then asked you why you feel like this, you would immediately start to talk about the sudden drop that turned your stomach, how you thought that the car would leave the track and send you plummeting to your death, about how the loop-the-loop or the corkscrew left your heart in your mouth, about how the sensation of speed and lack of control left you breathless.

While this is all true and gives us an image of how you experienced the ride, these are just snippets, highlights of your experience. If I am to really understand your experience, I need to understand your whole journey – both the physical, sensory journey and the emotional journey that it generated within you.

At the start of your journey there is a feeling of anticipation, maybe apprehension. The rollercoaster then starts its ascent up the first incline. Your anticipation increases. You hear a loud clicking sound, the car jerks a bit as it approaches the top, and your apprehension increases: Is the mechanism about to fail? Are you about to fall backward and crash back to the start at the bottom?

As the car reaches the top and begins its first descent, instead of being unnerved by the drop and acceleration, you are relieved that you didn't fall backward. The rollercoaster is not broken after all. It will be OK. After the increasing apprehension of the first ascent, this ride is turning out to be less frightening than you had thought. You relax a little. Then your car suddenly jerks round to the left - you are caught completely by surprise. Did it leave the rails, are you crashing? Before you have recovered your wits the car drops again - faster this time. Your stomach is left behind...

And so the ride goes on. There will be gentle, calming parts where you enjoy the view across the theme park and out to sea, and sudden twists, turns, and drops, some of which you anticipate or see coming and some of which catch you unawares.

But while the height and speed of the drops and the sharpness of the twists and turns are important, so is the emotional state that you are in as you enter each event. If you anticipated it or saw it coming, it is less disturbing than if you were caught off guard. If you were in a heightened state of nervousness as you hit that sudden bend or drop it will have a much greater effect on you.

While theme parks around the world compete for the highest, fastest, the most loop-the-loops, the rollercoasters that manage the riders' journeys the best give the best experience. These are the rides that build your anticipation before lulling you into a false sense of security, before dropping you over the edge.

It is the same with food and drink. It is not just about the flavors and the textures. It is about the journey that those flavors and textures take you on. While the key emotions of that journey are important, the subtleties in how it delivers those emotions are also critical. It is about how it moves you from each part of the experience to the next - the highs and lows of the experience, the sudden twists and turns, and your emotional preparedness for each of these transitions.

It is about the whole Shape of Taste.

As I said at the end of Chapter 2, understanding how and why you respond to certain aromas, tastes, and textures can be enlightening as to why you make some of the choices that you do and why you feel as you do about certain foods and drinks.

Understanding the Shape of Taste for whole groups or even populations can be vital for food manufacturers and for brand owners trying to develop and promote their food and drink brands across the world.

Ben and Jerry's in Japan

Ben and Jerry's, for example, was about to make a third attempt at launching into the rapidly developing ice cream market in Japan. Two previous attempts had been unsuccessful and this third one was not looking good, as all the research was telling the company that Japanese consumers did not like the 'bits' in its ice cream. This was a big problem for a brand that is predicated on the additions that it has in all its flavors.

The Marketing Clinic team was asked to go to Japan and find out what the real issue was and if Ben and Jerry's ice cream really was a nonstarter in this market. Alternatively, how could Ben and Jerry's turn this around and make its distinctive trademark 'additions' a successful differentiator in this market as it was elsewhere?

We profiled the emotional journeys of some of Ben and Jerry's and competitive flavors with consumers in Japan. Sitting in Tokyo eating ice cream – it was a tough job, but someone had to do it. What quickly became apparent was that it was not the 'bits' in themselves that the consumers disliked, but the journey that many of these bits took the consumers on.

Ben and Jerry's is an American brand and most of its flavors had been developed in America for Americans. You start with a sweet ice cream and add popular confectionery pieces into it. This gives you intense textural contrasts and a multi-stage consumption experience as the ice cream melts and you then chew or crunch the confectionery.

In most cases the additions are even sweeter than the ice cream and thus sweetness builds upon sweetness. In the US, Europe, and even in many Southeast Asian markets, this is generally regarded as an indulgence and is an integral part of consumers' love of the brand. In Japan, building sweetness is challenging. While the sweetness of ice cream was part of its attraction, when the additions built upon the sweetness it became too much for these consumers, who would then report that they liked the ice cream but not the bits.

We showed, however, that when savory or less sweet additions were added to the ice cream, the same Japanese consumers loved Ben and Jerry's – bits and all.

We then worked with the brand's team to draw up a list of existing flavors that would work in Japan, prioritizing the strongest as launch flavors. We also prepared a product development brief for potential new flavors. Following this work, Ben and Jerry's launched successfully into the Japanese market and now has a thriving mini-pot business and scoop shops across the country with a selection of global and US flavors alongside specific Japanese and Southeast Asian ones.

Positioning Nescafé in China

When Nescafé wanted to launch premium instant coffee into China, it needed specific knowledge about the emotional drivers for consumers there. China is traditionally a tea market with, at that time, little understanding of or interest in coffee. While the first Starbucks outlets were appearing on the streets of Beijing and Shanghai, these were frequented by visiting Westerners and largely ignored by the locals. Conventional research was telling Nescafé that Chinese consumers had no interest in, or need for, coffee. In fact, when our Marketing Clinic researchers arrived in Shanghai to start the project, we were met by a slightly bemused local team. "Why are you coming here to research coffee? We drink coffee on certain ritual occasions, but no one really likes it. We all prefer tea. It is not going to catch on here."

It wasn't as if they didn't know what coffee was. Many Chinese households, we heard, have a special coffee set hidden away somewhere at home. It was brought out when someone important came to visit and a traditional coffee ritual would be observed as a way of showing respect. But no one liked this coffee and why would anyone want to drink coffee instead of tea?

It was clear that, if we were offering coffee as an alternative to tea, there was little chance that an average Chinese consumer was going to be interested. However, that was not the intention of the team at Nescafé and that was not what we were in China to look at.

We started by researching what 'premium' meant to modern urban Chinese consumers. Throughout the first phase of research, we never mentioned coffee. We had no interest in the participants' thoughts about or preferences for tea or coffee at all. We talked about cars, computers, telephones, clothes, restaurants, anything that the respondent thought about when we asked questions around the subject of premiumness and their aspirations.

As these Chinese consumers told us their stories, we quickly built a picture of what premium meant to them, of what made one thing more premium than another. What motivated them to aspire to ownership of, or participation in, more premium products and activities, alongside which aspects of premiumness they did not find attractive or motivational.

It was after we had built up a comprehensive picture of the emotional drivers of premiumness for these consumers that we introduced some coffee into the groups. First the aroma and appearance of the coffee granules - color, size, shape - and eventually the consumption experience from aroma through to aftertaste. Again, we never asked the consumers what they liked or preferred. We simply profiled their emotional responses to understand which aspects of the coffee prompted the appropriate responses to suit a premium positioning of the coffee that Nescafé wanted to launch.

We were then able to go back to the Nescafé team with some exact recommendations for positioning, communications, appearance, and aroma of the grains, and a clear recommendation for a taste journey for a premium instant coffee to launch in China.

This coffee was successful, not because it was drunk instead of tea, but because it was premium. It was packaged and promoted as premium. It looked and smelt premium and, when drinking it, this coffee felt premium. By identifying and understanding the desire for premiumness and the drivers that made something feel premium for these consumers, and then making a coffee experience that delivered these emotions, we helped Nescafé to create a completely new market for coffee in China – one that has rapidly grown into a mature and very successful market for Nescafé and also for competitor brands.

What premiumness means in different cultures

We went on to develop a premium coffee in the Philippines. This was already a well-developed coffee market but one where competitive activity was driving prices down and squeezing profitability. The successful launch of a premium coffee in the Philippines segmented the coffee market there and helped Nescafé improve profitability.

What I have always remembered most about this project is the vastly differing attitudes that drive feelings of premiumness in the two countries.

We found that, in simple terms, there are four emotions that prompt feelings of premiumness:

- Aspiration: These are the things that I desire, that I wish to own or partake in. I will work hard so that I can achieve and enjoy these things.
- Indulgence: This makes me feel good; it is something that I enjoy. I deserve this.

- Competitiveness: I like this because it is better than the other options. This makes me look good; it shows that I am an achiever/better than others.
- Reassurance: This makes me feel more secure. It is better quality/more expensive so it must be better than the alternative. It is a safe choice.

In our experience with The Marketing Clinic, most people will, to some extent, be driven by all four and the extent to which any one or two is more dominant will vary between people, occasions, and even the types of product or activity being considered. However, whenever you look at an identifiable group such as a region, a nation, or a culture, you will find a clear pattern of dominance driving a cultural view of premiumness.

In China, where traditional Chinese culture is combined with rapid change, growth, and urbanization, competitiveness and reassurance dominated as the drivers of feelings of premium, while in the Philippines, indulgence and reassurance were the main drivers.

While Nescafé was ostensibly trying to achieve the same thing in each market – the launch of a premium coffee – these differences had to be recognized in the positioning and communication of that coffee and also in the taste journey. Two very different coffees and positionings were required to achieve what appeared to be much the same thing.

Chapter 1 established how we make our food and drink choices because of the way these choices make us feel; Chapter 2 showed how you can connect the sensorial journey with the emotional journey that it triggers; and in Chapter 3 I used real-life case studies to illustrate the importance of the consumer's emotional response over and above their rational response to flavor and texture. In Chapter 4, I have shown why the emotional journey – the Shape of Taste – is what differentiates brands from their competition.

Key ideas from this chapter

- While the endpoint is important, it's the journey that is the essence of the brand.

- It is not just about the flavors and the textures. It is about the journey that those flavors and textures take you on. It is about the whole Shape of Taste.

- Often the endpoint is a category benefit – all sodas are refreshing. It is the journey to the endpoint that differentiates a brand from its competitors.

- For Nescafé, launching a premium coffee in China and the Philippines, two very different coffees and positionings were required to achieve what appeared to be much the same thing.

Chapter 5

How the Shape of Taste helps to improve communications and advertising

Perceptions and expectations can have a significant effect on the emotional journey of consumption. In this chapter, you'll find out more about how advertising messages, previous experiences, and even what consumers read online can significantly affect their enjoyment of what they eat and drink.

When you are eating or drinking something, you never do this in total isolation. Your enjoyment of any food or drink is partly affected by your environment, by the company that you are with, by what you have previously consumed. As I well know, ouzo is great when on vacation in Greece, enjoyed with a loved one on a warm balcony overlooking the Aegean Sea. It never tastes quite as good on a cold winter's afternoon in Slough (an unremarkable town in southern England).

One of my favorite workshop tasks is to give participants strawberry-flavored chews that are colored blue. The audience are invariably food and drink professionals, but they rarely guess the flavor correctly. The blue color sets up expectations of the flavor and strawberry is not one of the possibilities. They are better at guessing the flavor blindfolded than when misled by the color.

Another, simpler way of playing the same game is with potato chips – not the obvious flavors that everyone is familiar with: Choose some less familiar ones. First try them without knowing their flavor. It can be hard to guess. Then try them again, having read the flavor description, and realize how you can now taste and recognize the subtleties of the flavor combinations that you could not identify before.

This is not because you are not good at identifying tastes. It is because your brain uses a variety of information sources and pieces them all together to help you understand what you are tasting.

The color, the aroma, the texture all set up expectations before the taste is even considered. Other information such as flavor descriptions or previous experience will also affect these expectations. Have you ever taken a sip or a bite of something and reeled back at the taste because it was not what you expected? The shock is often not because it tasted bad, but simply that the flavor was different from what you were prepared for.

As an example, if a friend tells you they tried a new chocolate bar last week and think you might like it, you may be tempted to try it yourself. When you do, you will start with the expectation that it will be good – your friend recommended it and you trust their judgment. You may be intrigued by the packaging, by its appearance, and these may give you further clues as to what it might taste like and its texture. As you bite into the bar, there may be some textural and maybe some flavor surprise – you may like these revelations, you may not. However, your friend thought you would like this and they were right. It's good.

How would you feel if, as you bit into it, you didn't like it at all? Disappointed!

Disappointed in the chocolate bar, but also in your friend's judgment.

If you had discovered the chocolate bar on your own and

didn't like it, that would have been disappointing, but your expectations were heightened by your friend's recommendation, so the disappointment is that much greater.

Imagine then that your friend had not just said they thought you would like it, but it was the best thing they had ever tasted and you would absolutely love it as well. Now your anticipation is set at a high level. The chocolate bar must now meet your elevated expectations to deliver on this promise. If, as you bite into the bar, it tastes OK – pleasant, enjoyable, but not very different from other chocolate bars – you will feel at least a little disappointed. What would have been a pleasant chocolate bar if you had discovered it without any recommendation, or even if your friend had just said they thought you might like it, is now disappointing. It is the same chocolate bar. The only difference was your expectation.

Brands occasionally forget this. In their desire to entice consumers to try their new, improved, or different product, they sometimes go a little too far in telling them how wonderful it is.

Most of us can probably think of a product where the advertising has spoken to us – promising a superb taste experience, an explosion of flavor that will invigorate and recharge us, or a luxurious melt that will calm and slow us down, enveloping us in a wave of indulgence – only to then find the product quite prosaic. It's pleasant, even nice, but ultimately disappointing compared with the promise.

To be fair, the best advertising is much more sophisticated than this. It recognizes that every consumption experience generates an emotional change in the consumer – that we are partial to a product because it makes us feel better than we did before we consumed it. Advertising tries to communicate the emotions of the consumption experience rather than the consumption experience itself, and associate the product with both the occasion and the improved emotional state – whether it's Snickers showing how people are not at their best when they're hungry and how a Snickers always makes things better, or Nescafé suggesting that sitting together over coffee brings us together "for the moments that matter."

Good advertising, well executed, but is it the best message? Snickers vs Nescafé

These advertisements are successful because they are based on a truth and the relevant products do help facilitate the mood change. Most of us are not at our best when hungry, and sitting together over coffee is usually a great shared experience. A Snickers bar relieves hunger and Nescafé creates sociable moments for people to talk and get to know each other better. These brands are – successfully – taking ownership of an occasion and positioning their brand as the best solution.

But why is Snickers better than any other chocolate bar, or any other snack, at filling the gap when you are hungry? And what makes Nescafé the best coffee for bringing us together?

Snickers will argue it is because the bar contains nuts and so is more filling. A closer examination of consumers' emotional responses to eating a Snickers confirms this – most consumers would agree that a Snickers is the most substantial, most filling chocolate bar (this is about their emotional response to eating the bar, not a literal comparison of actual calories). The Snickers ads talk about the nuts: They direct the consumer's attention to the nuts and associate them with the ability of a Snickers to make you feel better. When consumers eat a Snickers bar, the 'truth' of the advertising message is confirmed in their own minds. When they eat a different chocolate bar, there are no nuts: It feels less substantial, less filling.

Snickers can, and does, take ownership of that occasion. If you are hungry and that hunger is getting in the way of you being at your best, a Snickers bar is the answer.

However, compare this with the Nescafé example. It is true that sitting down with family or friends and enjoying a

Nescafé together is a great experience. Nescafé is great "for the moments that matter", for bringing us together. But why is Nescafé any better for these occasions than any other coffee, or even tea? Why is it better, more enjoyable, more unifying, than Jacobs, a Starbucks, or a Costa Coffee?

There is nothing in the Nescafé ads to differentiate it from other coffees. It is an advertising message that has been very successful at taking ownership of these occasions in many markets around the world, but it leaves the brand vulnerable. The ads are promoting a generic, category-wide benefit, but giving the consumer no reason to believe that Nescafé is better than its competitors.

When Nescafé has a dominant share of the instant coffee category in a particular market, it benefits most from simply growing that overall market. But if a competitor or new entrant into the market gives the consumer a reason to believe that its coffee is better – that it has a better aroma, a smoother taste, a stronger flavor – and the consumer finds this to be 'true' in their consumption experience, then the competitor can quickly take share from Nescafé.

Advertising should intrigue the consumer. It should offer them something a little bit different, something attractive, enticing. The best advertisements tug at your emotions rather than offering logical reasons why you should try the product. They must be motivational enough to either confirm your current behavior (make you stay with the brand) or change your behavior (make you try a new brand).

When you then try the brand, it must deliver on the promise of the ad. There must be a truth in the consumption experience that confirms what you thought you understood the advertisement was saying to you. If the advertisement is to create loyalty to a specific brand rather than just grow the overall market, then that 'truth' must be unique and ownable. To draw, perhaps a little too heavily, on the Snickers example, the brand must have some 'nuts.'

This is where I have seen so many brands get it wrong. As Chapter 3 reinforced, the endpoint of the consumer journey – how the product makes them feel after consuming it – is important, but this is often a generic category benefit. All chocolate bars fill you up; all coffees are great sociable drinks.

The essence of a brand is in the journey that it takes you on to get to that endpoint. It is the rollercoaster ride, Hitchcock's green script. The endpoint is the reason that consumers buy into the category, the reason that they buy a chocolate bar or a coffee. But the reason they choose Snickers or Nescafé is because of the unique way that they deliver the consumer to that endpoint – their unique journey.

If they are to build their brand, brand owners must focus on the consumer's emotional journey. Focusing only on the endpoint builds the category – all coffees – rather than their own market share.

To draw a simple analogy – you can think about a brand as a vehicle to move the consumer from mood A to mood B. No car manufacturer advertises their car as the best way to get from A to B. They all talk about how great it feels to travel in their car.

Changing the message, not the product

When a brand is struggling, it is easy for a brand owner to get drawn into focusing on the wrong thing. Invariably they are not doing anything wrong. In fact, they are probably doing exactly what the corporate guidelines say they should be doing and what anyone else in their position would too. But that is the problem. On the other side of the battle for market share is another brand owner. They are either behaving in the same way, so the two brands are locked in a stalemate. Or they are breaking the rules – or operating to a different set of rules – so that, despite the struggling brand doing all the right things, it is still losing share.

The Marketing Clinic was asked to help out in just such a

case in South Africa. Our client had a great global brand that held market leadership positions in almost every market in which it operated. In South Africa, it had always been well ahead of the competition, but recently a local competitor had been taking chunks out of its share. This competitor was now starting to discount its product and taking even more share.

Our client had done all the proper things: The team had improved the product, making it even better than the competitor, and had run some great brand-building advertising. But every time the competitor put its product on offer, our client lost more market share. Whatever our client did to try to build the brand, the competitor's actions seemed to be further commoditizing the market. The battle was turning into a trading and price war with margins becoming increasingly eroded.

The client asked us to look at the situation. What further product improvements, the client wanted to know, did it need to make to rebuild its brand values, to gain preference for its brand against the competition and to regain market share and a price advantage against the competitor?

We quickly discovered that our client's product was already preferred by most consumers. Further than this, past product 'improvements' had in fact undermined the historic trust and belief in the brand, rather than improving perceptions of it.

There were several competitive products that might be used in place of our brand, but all except one were perceived to be nowhere near as good. The one that was thought to be nearly as good was exactly that: It was nearly as good. Unlike the rest of the competitors, it was in the same league as our product and comparable. Unfortunately, partly because the traditional belief in our brand had been undermined by product changes and partly because of financial pressures, 'nearly as good' was good enough for many.

However, once we understood the sensory difference

between the brands and what emotional triggers this difference fired, it became quite straightforward to communicate this difference to the consumers. Rationally, most consumers already knew that our product tasted better. But when we expressed this difference in emotional terms, when we highlighted the Shape of Taste and emotional journey of our product, suddenly it started to mean something important to the consumers. Now they could articulate why our product was better.

They started to notice the difference every time they used either our brand or the competitor. Now they understood and could articulate the difference. Now they noticed how it made them feel. Now that difference was important to them.

Our recommendation was that the client did not change the product, but that they changed their advertising to highlight this emotional journey – to highlight the key emotional moments to consumers so they would notice them when they consumed our product, and the lack of this emotional journey when they tried the competitor product. Within weeks of actioning these recommendations, more and more consumers started to say they preferred and would buy our brand and market share started heading back upwards.

Subtle changes in communication can make a big difference

Cornetto is a global ice cream brand and the leading brand in its sector in just about every market in which it operates. As with all leading brands, it is targeted by other global brands and by local brands in each market. The Cornetto team asked us to help them understand more about what makes Cornetto great and how they could improve their product and communication to keep it ahead of the competition.

What was really interesting as we researched Cornetto and its competitors in Europe and in Asia was that there were competitors that were cheaper, but consumers were willing to pay more for Cornetto. There were competitors that had better quality ice cream, more additions, more luxury versions, but Cornetto was always more popular. It was not the quality of the ice cream, it was not the number or the indulgence of the additions that made the difference. It was the sensorial and emotional journey that the ice creams took their consumers along that differentiated them.

We identified a specific number of different stages in the consumption experience of Cornetto. Each different stage prompted a different emotional response from the consumer, and the order and relative intensity of each stage delivered a unique overall emotional journey. We discovered that not only do the competitors not have as many stages in their consumption experience but, even more importantly, the relative intensities of the stages they do have and the transitions between the stages do not transport the consumer through a smooth, enticing journey in anything like the same way that Cornetto does. Cornetto delivers a unique emotional journey that is highly attractive to its target market. Not only this, but when Cornetto is eaten by groups or couples, this journey unites them, brings them together, in a way that the competitors just do not achieve.

Following this research, we were able to advise the Cornetto team on some subtle nuances in their communication strategy. Their advertising agency had developed a communications strategy based on 'fearless romance'. The interpretation of fearless romance, however, was not differentiating the brand from competitor products also aimed at the same young age cohort.

When the emotional journey of Cornetto is understood, it is clear that Cornetto brings people together. Remembering the Ancient Greeks' definitions of love, Cornetto should be *philia*, not *eros*: friendship or affection - bringing people together - rather than romantic love. This insight led to subtle changes in the communications strategy that created a differentiated space for Cornetto – one that feels true for consumers when they eat the ice cream.

This detailed understanding of the Cornetto consumption experience also led to a tighter focus on product development directions. It allowed the team to turn their attention away from worrying about the quality of ice cream or the number of additions of their competitors, to focus on what made the Cornetto brand great – the consumption journey – and creating variations of that.

NRG: taking Lucozade from health drink to energy drink

I include this as a great marketing case study that explains how changing your positioning and communications can transform a brand. However, I can claim no credit as I was still at school when the work was done on this one.

When I was a child in the 1970s, if I had been ill, my mother would buy me a bottle of Lucozade. It came in a glass bottle wrapped in yellow cellophane. With the advertising slogan "Lucozade aids recovery", it was generally purchased in a pharmacy. It was also a regular gift from hospital visitors to recuperating friends and family. However, even then, the brand was in decline. The British population was becoming healthier, incidences of illness less frequent, annual epidemics of flu less common.

In 1978, the brand attempted to move away from illness towards being a healthy provider of energy to help people recover from the natural daily lulls they might suffer during their day. However, this repositioning was still rooted in health and recovery and was of limited success.

In 1982, the brand repositioned again. It dropped the glass bottle and the cellophane wrapper and moved to a plastic (PET) bottle. It ditched the "aids recovery" slogan and replaced it with "Lucozade replaces lost energy". Lucozade became a brand that could provide energetic, busy, and successful people with the energy they needed to perform to their full potential. Brand decline was reversed and Lucozade went from strength to strength. In 1990, Lucozade Sport was launched, becoming the UK's first mainstream sports drink and creating a new market that was worth more than £3 billion in 2022.

Although the repositioning from a sickness recovery drink to a sports drink is significant, it should be clear to any observer that the emotional shift delivered by the drink is very much the same. When I drank Lucozade as a child lying under a blanket on the couch in my parents' living room recovering from a bout of sickness, I felt the energy flowing into me, I felt stronger, I felt better and more able to carry on. Now as I drink Lucozade Sport when riding my bike up yet another hill, it may be a completely different product, but I can feel the energy flowing into me; I feel stronger, better, and more able to carry on.

In 2013, GSK sold Lucozade (along with Ribena) for £1.35 billion – a clear win in finding a renewed positioning for an outdated product.

Transforming a category: fruit and herbal infusions in the UK

Lucozade is now so well established as a sports and energy drink that its transformation seems quite obvious in hindsight. This is true of many of the best insights, which seem to be obvious only after they have been brought to light and explained in detail. This becomes even more the case when the insights in question lead to a structural change in the way that a whole category is positioned and communicated.

We had carried out several successful projects with Twinings when its team spoke to us about a problem with their fruit and herbal tea ranges. The brand had a handful of highly successful and popular flavors but also a huge tail of less successful ones. However, whenever any of these less popular flavors were delisted by a supermarket, or Twinings withdrew a flavor, the company would receive impassioned letters from a few consumers who loved the flavor that had been withdrawn. Twinings knew that its teas were good. It knew that once consumers discovered them, they loved them. But whatever it tried, sales continued to focus on the best-known varieties.

As we looked into consumer responses to the range of infusions on offer, we quickly realized that it came down to that all-important question: "Why do people drink these teas?"

Consumers drink fruit and herbal infusions not just because they are thirsty, or because they have reached that time of the day. They choose fruit and herbal teas because they derive a greater benefit from them. They perceive them to be healthier, wholesome; these teas make consumers feel more hydrated, more energized, more relaxed, cleansed.

As we profiled the range of fruit and herbal teas, we began to understand not only which teas triggered which feelings of specific health benefits – which flavors relaxed and calmed, which energized, which nourished – but also what it was about their consumption experiences that prompted these beliefs.

While there was a general association of some flavors with specific benefits (chamomile tea as calming), this was more to do with traditional associations with the herb or fruit rather than any understanding of the consumption experience. Our research meant that we were able to give the Twinings team, for the first time, a comprehensive understanding of the perceived effect of each infusion through the range. This enabled them to organize the range by perceived benefit rather than by flavor, as they had done previously.

Shortly after this, Twinings relaunched its fruit and herbal infusions grouped by benefit – Calming Relaxing, Sleep Time, Cleansing, Invigorating – rather than by category (herbal teas, fruit teas). Consumers could now select their teas for the benefits they were looking for and, when seeking alternative flavors, choose the right ones for the occasion – thus avoiding potential disappointment.

This proved to be so successful (even intuitive when viewed with hindsight) that shortly afterward the supermarket own brands and other competitors followed Twinings' lead. Subsequently, the way that the UK market viewed fruit and herbal infusions changed completely.

This chapter has shown how perceptions and expectations affect the emotional response to a product and underlines the importance of the communication and positioning of a brand in how consumers respond to it. When a brand team understands the Shape of Taste of their product, they can be much more effective in how they position and communicate their brand.

Key ideas from this chapter

⁍ When you try the brand, it must deliver on the promise of the ad. There must be a truth in the consumption experience that confirms what you thought you understood the advertisement was saying to you.

⁍ If the advertisement is to create loyalty to a specific brand, rather than just grow the overall market, then that 'truth' must be unique and ownable.

⁍ Brand owners must focus on the consumer's emotional journey if they are to build their brand. Focusing on just the endpoint builds the category (all coffees) rather than their own market share.

⁍ You can think about a brand as a vehicle to move the consumer from mood A to mood B. No car manufacturer advertises their car as the best way to get from A to B. They all talk about how great it feels to travel in their car.

Chapter 6

Diving deeper into complexity

In the earlier part of this book, I discussed how, as humans, our physiological experiences trigger emotional journeys - that certain aromas, flavors, textures, experiences are paired with memories, and when we experience these sensory aspects they trigger an emotional response. The previous three chapters have explored, through case studies of The Marketing Clinic's work with brands, how you can use this knowledge to create better products and communicate them more effectively to consumers. However, it is, of course, rarely that simple.

In this chapter, I discuss how to approach the complexity of flavors and textures and the emotions that they evoke, how the human brain deals with this complexity, and what this means for taste experts such as tea and coffee tasters and for psychologists such as myself. You'll see why grasping this complexity is crucial in understanding the Shape of Taste. I will also offer some insights into why people dunk biscuits.

The multiple layers of sensorial experience

Nearly every sensorial experience is multifaceted. Any food or drink has more than just one flavor. I discussed this when thinking about coffee in Chapter 2, but also listen to any wine expert describing a French Malbec or a New Zealand Sauvignon Blanc. Their language may be flowery, but it does capture the complexity and delight to be found in just a sip of wine, and this is equally true of almost anything that you eat or drink, should you care to pause and think about it.

Textures also change as we eat, breaking down from hard to soft, from crunchy to chewy, from crumbly to melting. Many favorite foods combine different textures, with crispy outsides and soft centers, or a chewy consistency with crunchy bits.

If the sensorial experience of a product is complex and changing, then logically so is the emotional response to it. If you are receiving multiple and evolving stimuli, presumably your emotional reactions are also complex and changing. If this is the case, then how is it possible to attribute a single emotional journey – a single Shape of Taste – to the product, and how do you know which of the multiple stimuli the consumer is responding to and why?

The human brain is brilliant at dealing with complexity. It receives billions of messages every second – so many that we cannot consciously process and be aware of them all. Our subconscious mind processes and prioritizes these messages and we are consciously aware of only a very small proportion of them. These tend to be the important ones. Thus, we notice if something changes – how often have you become consciously aware of a background noise (for example, a fridge humming) only when it suddenly stops, or you only noticed that deer in the woods when it moved, even though you were looking straight at it only seconds before. It's not that you couldn't see or hear these things; it's just that you didn't notice them.

The same is true of your senses of taste, touch, and smell.

Your subconscious mind sorts the multitude of stimuli that you receive and you notice what is new, different, changing, challenging, or alarming. If you sit in a room for a while with a scented candle or air freshener, after a while you may stop noticing the aroma. But if you leave the room, and especially if you go outside into fresh air and then return, there it is – you may even think it's getting a little too strong and blow out the candle. Your conscious mind ignores what it deems to be less important – things that are not changing, the consistency in your environment – and notices the changes.

When hit with a multitude of data, the brain sorts it in a way that helps you to process, interpret, and understand it. When you take a sip of wine or cola, when you take a bite of a chocolate bar or a mouthful of dinner, you are immediately assaulted with a multitude of flavors, textures, aromas... the complexity of which is totally baffling. How do you make any sense of this? How do you break this complexity down into identifiable flavors?

Your brain sorts it for you, connecting what you see and smell with the flavors and textures that you experience. There are five flavors that have been identified (sweet, sour, salt, bitter, and umami). These flavors are complemented by the aromas that you sense through your retro-nasal cavity as you chew and by the textures you can feel. Subconsciously, your brain collects all this data together, orders it, and presents you with the information in a way that makes sense and that you can understand.

How your brain does this – and the fact that you perceive your taste experience in a way that is not necessarily the same as the way that you actually experience it – is demonstrated by the following story and experiment.

When I was at school, many more years ago than I care to remember, I was taught that the taste buds on your tongue are in zones. On the tip of the tongue are the taste buds sensitive to sweet flavors. Also towards the front are taste buds that register salt. Those at the edges note sourness, and bitter flavors are picked up at the back of the tongue. When I was at school, umami did not even exist (or certainly not in a British context).

These were reasonably self-evident 'facts'. Try it for yourself. If you pay attention as you eat, you can sense that this is how you taste your food. You can taste sweetness on the tip of your tongue and saltiness just behind it. Sour is at the sides (just suck a lemon or taste a spoonful of vinegar and the sides of your tongue will ache with the sourness), and bitter is at the back of the mouth, often peaking just as you swallow.

But now we know better. V B Collings debunked this myth as early as 1974, although it took a while to reach the school curriculum.

Taste buds are not as specialized as was previously thought. All taste buds register all flavors, sending very similar messages back to the brain. So, the zoning of the taste buds that you experienced if you tried the taste experiment two paragraphs ago is just the way that your brain sorts and presents this information. You perceive the tastes to be zoned in this way, even though there is no scientific reason for this to be so.

And so we get to one of the most interesting questions of psychology – in fact, even of philosophy. If we can demonstrate that our perception of an event is different from its actual occurrence, then which is most important: the way that we perceive it, or the way that it actually occurs?

The answer, I think, is that it depends on your perspective and what you are trying to achieve.

If you are a biochemist seeking to understand taste, stimuli, the workings of our biochemical receptors such as our taste buds, I expect you are much more interested in what is actually happening. But if you are just trying to enjoy your food, or you are a food psychologist, a brand manager, or a product developer for a food company, you are likely to be more interested in our perception of taste and flavor and our response to it rather than the precise biochemistry behind it.

So, when, with our research at The Marketing Clinic, we are dealing with the complexities of different stimuli and consumers' emotional responses to them, we look at people's perceived experience, the way that they feel it, rather than the scientifically accurate actual experience. This has interesting consequences.

Tea and coffee tasting: scientific accuracy or consumer perceptions?

Tea blenders are a highly skilled and incredibly well-informed lot. They can tell you not only about the different attributes of different tea plants and how these are characterized in the taste of the tea, but also how the soil type, the altitude, even the season and the weather affect the properties of each crop. The role of the tea blender is to take all this natural variety and complexity and produce a branded product that will make a cup of tea that tastes the same every time. They are constantly altering the exact blend of the product to rebalance the vagaries of natural variation and serve consumers a consistent cup of tea.

Their tasting skills are fantastic. There is plenty of science that goes into achieving the consistent cup of tea but, in the end, it comes down to the tasting skills of the blenders. I have worked with some of them (and coffee blenders too) and their understanding of flavor and of taste, their ability to spot and interpret minute subtleties, and their knowledge of how to balance them astounds me.

These specialists work in tasting labs. The tea is made with a precisely measured amount of water at a precise temperature, with exactly the right amount of tea leaf steeped for exactly the right length of time. If you are going to spot subtle differences, then consistency is important.

They taste it, of course, without any adulterations such as milk or sugar, and their tasting method is precise. You take a spoonful of the tea, you lift it to your lips, and you suck the contents of the spoon into your mouth with a sharp slurp. The idea is that the liquid is immediately and evenly distributed around your whole mouth. Once this is done the tea is then spat out into a spittoon.

This is the way to spot incredibly subtle differences in balance and taste, to achieve consistency, and deliver a quality branded product. It is not, however, how the consumer experiences the product. Tasting in this way generates a true understanding of the flavor and complexities of the product (whether tea, coffee, or wine). It tells us nothing, however, about the consumer's reaction to their experience of drinking it.

On occasion, I have walked into a tasting lab to speak with the blenders about the consumer experience. If this is the topic of conversation, I say to them that we need to make a few changes to their usual way of doing things. We need to drink the tea like the consumer drinks it. So, please can we have some proper mugs and some milk and sugar, and move away from the spittoon – because if you don't drink the tea, you don't experience the aftertaste or the feel of it flowing down your esophagus. We will talk about the way that the consumer perceives the flavor of the tea, despite the fact that these professionals know this to be just a perception and not a fact.

I love these conversations. I always learn so much more about the product, about the importance of balancing the acidity, about where the bitterness comes from, and how and why the temperature of the water and the time that the tea is steeped for affects the flavor. But I like to think that I also impart a much greater understanding about how what they do affects the consumer response to the product: why some variability in one area will never be noticed by the consumer while minimal variance in another may be critical to how they perceive the product.

To produce a great cup of tea, you need to understand the science and the true taste of the product. To understand the consumer's reaction to the tea, you need to understand their perception of the taste and flavors.

Unraveling the complexities, understanding the sequences

It is the complexity of the sensorial experience and the ways that you perceive the taste journey that make the psychology of food and drink so interesting. Each mouthful takes you on a journey. Every item that you munch or devour has a complexity of flavors and textures, though you do not experience them all in one big hit together but as a sequence. Far more important than the flavors and textures is the way that you experience that sequence.

A soda may start gently with a soft, simple sweetness, which is then cut as the carbonation becomes more apparent. Maybe it finishes with a complexity of flavors from its different ingredients or perhaps a degree of sourness that lasts into the aftertaste.

As discussed earlier, a Milky Way starts with a substantial bite, a hard crispy shell, then a soft center releasing more immediate flavors that flood through the mouth. As the flavorful center melts away, the initial peak of flavor disappears and the crispier, less flavorsome shell clears the mouth. The aftertaste is of the shell, but the memory of the peak of flavor from the center is strong and makes the product very moreish as the consumer seeks to re-experience this peak.

These are relatively simple journeys, but even with these the consumer's emotional response is driven as much by the order of the sequencing and the nature of the transitions – the heights of the peaks and the depths of the troughs – as by the flavor and textural experiences themselves.

It is fairly easy just to monitor and even measure someone's emotional response to a consumption experience, but to really understand that response you need to understand how and why it is prompted by the sequencing of the experience and by the transitions within that sequence.

Take a cup of coffee

One of my favorite contradictions in the world of food and drink is coffee, and it provides a great example of this.

As I discussed in Chapter 2, coffee is a great stimulant. It wakes you up, gets you going, helps you to refocus, re-energizes you when you are flagging. The smell of coffee, the first sip, and you are feeling better. But it takes 20 minutes for any caffeine to reach the bloodstream, so anything before that is in fact a placebo, an emotional and not a physiological reaction. That, however, does not make it any less effective.

Coffee is also a relaxing drink – great to sit with and chat to friends, a wonderful after-dinner drink when relaxing after a meal, something to take your time over and enjoy. So how can the same cuppa – and I do mean exactly the same brand, made in the same way – drunk on different occasions, fulfill completely opposite tasks?

It's all in the emotional response to the complexities of the taste journey. It is in the Shape of Taste.

Bitterness in coffee grabs your attention; it wakes you up and stimulates you. But it's not just the intensity of bitterness; it's also the way it is delivered. Is the bitterness immediate, as soon as the coffee enters the mouth, or does it build as the coffee moves through the mouth? Does it build suddenly or gradually? Is the bitterness a coarse, single-dimensional bitterness, or is it part of a more complex, multifaceted flavor? Does the bitterness last into the aftertaste or fade before the coffee is swallowed? These things all make a difference to the way the coffee stimulates. They also have a significant effect on how it can be relaxing.

In our work on coffee at The Marketing Clinic, we have consistently seen that if a sip of coffee is immediately bitter and stimulating and then that bitterness suddenly drops away, the consumer is calmed and relaxed as the intensity of the flavor eases. Or if the coffee has a more complex, multifaceted flavor, the consumer will be slowed to appreciate that complexity, and this too will have a calming, relaxing effect. The degree to which a coffee is stimulating and the degree to which it is relaxing and soothing is dependent not only on the flavors but also on the juxtaposition of how they are delivered.

The best coffees deliver a balance between stimulation and calming. They do this in different ways, varying between complexities in flavor and managing the way that the bitterness is delivered. The consumer then unconsciously chooses to take out of their consumption experience the emotions they are seeking at the time. When drinking coffee in the morning, they focus on its intensity and bitterness and thus find it awakening and stimulating. When drinking the same coffee after dinner with friends, they slow down and focus more on its flavor and complexity and so find it more relaxing and calming.

Why does this work? Because of the power of suggestion – the psychological process by which a person guides their desired thoughts, feelings, and behaviors into becoming reflexes instead of relying on conscious effort.

Ever since coffee houses opened up across Europe in the 17th century, coffee has been valued for being both stimulating and relaxing, so consumers today have no problem deriving which, or even both, of the conflicting emotional takeaways they are looking for at any specific time.

The complexities of vodka

"The ideal vodka is colorless, odorless, and tasteless," I was being told. If I had heard such a statement from anyone else, I would have taken it as a matter of personal opinion. If that was what they preferred, who was I to argue? But this was the gentleman who was going to be responsible for the development and manufacture of the vodka that I was developing a taste brief for with The Marketing Clinic.

This was in 2010, and we had started in St Petersburg, moved north of the Arctic Circle into Murmansk, then worked our way south through Moscow, Penza, and into Krasnodar near the Black Sea. Our brief was to develop a mass-market vodka that would be popular across Russia – not just regionally, as was the case for most mass-market brands at that time. This conversation confirmed something that we already suspected from the way that our host spoke disparagingly about Russian vodkas and admiringly about Western vodkas, and jealously guarded a bottle of Grey Goose (which is French) while happily sharing out the Russian brands. Although Russian himself, he aspired to Western brands, rejected his own heritage, and had lost touch with the market that he was supposed to be supplying. We clearly had a task ahead of us – not only to find a taste profile that worked from the frozen north to the warm sunny climes of the south, but also to convince our host that he needed to produce something that his consumers wanted, rather than tell them what he thought they should want.

The trick was in understanding the emotional journey of the Russian consumers when they drank vodka, and how the consumption experience delivered that emotional journey. Then, while doing this, we had to understand what was different about the emotional requirement in Murmansk, where the sun did not rise on some winter days, and in Krasnodar, which has a latitude similar to that of Venice or Lyon. How could we deliver the different emotional requirements from the same liquor?

As we investigated the most desired emotional journey of vodka, it soon became apparent that while a similar set of emotions was experienced throughout the country, the balance of the way in which they were delivered changed as you moved south. Consumers in Murmansk and St Petersburg craved a more aggressive delivery, while the southerners of Krasnodar were a little more laid back. In Murmansk, the locals would add Tabasco to their shot to increase the kick and the warmth, while in St Petersburg and Moscow they sought out more subtle flavors and drank their vodka in slightly different ways.

Once we understood this and could identify the sensorial qualities that delivered the different emotions, we could also explain to our host why certain brands sold better in each region. He started to become convinced when he realized that we could tell him which brands sold in which region just by tasting them and without any sales knowledge.

Far from a colorless, odorless, tasteless liquid, Russian consumers are looking for a mixture of tastes and sensations from their vodka. A ubiquitous national brand would have to strike a very delicate balance, delivering warmth and aggression as well as complexity of flavor and some soothing, calming emotions.

The talent is in managing the key attributes of the drink to deliver the quintessential emotions – not just the warmth that the consumer feels, but also the way that the warmth accrues through the experience and the impression of pace in the drink as it moves through the mouth. This may seem meaningless when vodka is drunk as a shot, but just try a Polish potato vodka and compare that to an American wheat vodka and you will experience the difference in pace. Then there is the delivery of flavor: not just the nature of the flavor, but where it occurs in the experience – its juxtaposition with the delivery of the heat and how the flavor comes and goes as the shot moves through the mouth and the throat.

We were able to deliver a brief for a category-busting national brand of vodka, but in addition, and at least as importantly, we were able to convince our host that vodka should be so much more than a colorless, odorless, and tasteless liquid.

Why do people dunk cookies?

We have carried out several research studies over the years to understand the complexities of biscuits. (I've written biscuits here because I am English – if you are American, I mean cookies.) I love working on biscuits. Apart from the fact that I enjoy eating some of the samples, they are a fascinating topic. If I asked you to name ten things that you get excited about, biscuits would probably not be on your list. If, however, you ask a group of people to each answer the question, "If you could only have one type of biscuit for the rest of your life, which would you choose?", the conversation will soon hot up. And you might be surprised by some of the choices!

Typically, biscuits are crunchy and crumbly at first and then the crumbs – and the chocolate or cream if they have some – melt in the mouth. This means they are energizing and awakening first and then comforting, relaxing, and reassuring. This, in turn, has a significant effect on the way in which they are regarded by the consumer and the types of occasions on which they are eaten.

But if each of these stages – crispy and crumbly and then the melt – is important to the consumer reaction (and they are), then what happens when the biscuit is dunked into a hot drink? The consumption experience has now been completely changed. The biscuit enters the mouth wet and soggy. You bypass the crispy, crumbly stage altogether and just have the melt.

If you focus on the consumption journey, dunking a biscuit creates quite a different experience from eating it without dunking. Sensorially, a biscuit dunked in a cup of tea is a very different experience to a biscuit without a drink. However, if you focus on the consumer's emotional journey, you can see it in another way.

Without dunking, the crispy, crumbly experience in the first phase of biscuit consumption awakens and stimulates the consumer, while the melt calms, relaxes, and reassures them. When dunking a biscuit, attention is required. Dunking requires the consumer's full concentration, or it ends in disaster. Thus, the consumer is distracted from whatever else they are doing. Their attention is focused on the dunking; they are awakened and excited. The dunked biscuit then melts in the mouth - the consumer is soothed, relaxed, reassured.

The same emotional journey has been achieved in a different way.

So, the complexity of the experience and the way in which the brain sequences the physiological experience is important in the emotional response that it evokes. This is what the Shape of Taste depicts and explains. When brand owners focus on the emotional journey of their products and on the Shape of Taste rather than the taste itself, they can think differently about product and communications developments.

Key ideas from this chapter

🍴 If we can demonstrate that our perception of an event is different from its actual occurrence, then which is most important: the way in which we perceive it, or the way it actually occurs?

🍴 To produce a great food or beverage product, you need to understand the science and the true taste of the product. To understand the consumer's reaction to the product, you need to understand their perception of the flavors and textures.

🍴 Each mouthful takes you on a journey. You experience flavors and textures as a sequence. Far more important than what the flavors and textures are is the way that you experience that sequence.

🍴 The consumer's emotional response to their consumption experience is driven as much by the order of the sequencing of flavors and textures and the nature of the transitions – the heights of the peaks and the depths of the troughs – as by the flavor and textural experiences themselves.

🍴 Russian vodka should not be colorless, odorless, and tasteless.

🍴 Sensorially, a biscuit dunked in a cup of tea is a very different experience to a biscuit without a drink. But focusing on the consumer's emotional journey, you can see that when you dunk biscuits, you achieve the same emotional journey in a different way.

Chapter 7

Belief is vital

This chapter is not about religion. It is, however, about the faith and belief that consumers have in products and brands.

Brands were created as a shorthand way to communicate so much more about a product than just what it is. They evoke a belief and a trust in the quality and reliability of the product and increasingly in the company behind the product, its processes and production methods, in its ethics, its sustainability, and in what it stands for. However, a consumer's faith and belief in a brand can be a precarious thing and they rely not just on what the brand says to them but also in the 'truth' that they feel when they consume it.

Clearly communication has a lot to do with what people believe. If your doctor or nutritionist tells you that you should eat oatmeal for breakfast to help reduce your cholesterol and keep you going until lunchtime, then you are more likely to believe it than if you saw it in an advertisement for any particular brand of porridge oats.

However, once you are converted to the idea of oats for breakfast, how will you choose which ones to eat? Maybe you are driven by convenience and will choose a ready-to-eat, instant, or microwavable porridge. You may want a more natural product and seek out a less processed option, or you find oats bland and want something flavored or that has additions to make it more interesting. Gradually, the layers of expectation of your new breakfast are building. You started out looking for a healthier breakfast; now you also want it to be quick to prepare, natural, and flavorsome.

Once you choose your product and start to eat, it must deliver on all these levels. You may be willing to accept some compromise between naturalness and flavor or between convenience and naturalness, but each compromise, each lack of delivery, is a disappointment. If the product fails to deliver too many of your expectations, it's going to take a huge amount of willpower to maintain this healthier breakfast regime, whatever the doctor said.

But the interesting question about even this simple example is: What do we mean by the product 'delivering' on these expectations?

Your original motivation to change your breakfast to oats was to improve your health. It may be enough that your doctor or nutritionist told you that this would be the case, but most of us need to actually *feel* better for the change – not just to be told that it is good for us. There needs to be something in the eat, the aftertaste, the way it feels in your stomach, that prompts you to *believe*, and continue to believe every time you eat it, that this is a healthier breakfast. You need to sense some positive associations and develop a positive feedback loop if you are to stick to your new breakfast regime.

I will come back to what these prompts might be – to what it is about the eating experience that might make you believe this is a healthier breakfast. But before I do, despite health being your main motivator, you are unlikely to convert to oats for breakfast unless they also fulfill the other criteria I mentioned, such as naturalness, convenience, and flavor.

For the purpose of this book, I won't delve too deeply into what you might mean by 'naturalness' or 'convenient', but a quick look will give an idea of how complex this is becoming. In the case of naturalness, the pack and the advertising can tell you how 'natural' the product is. It may even look more natural than other products. But if you are going to believe that this is a more natural product, there must be something in the consumption experience that prompts this. The product should 'feel' more natural as you eat it. And, while flavor is another of your criteria, this flavor should add to, rather than contradict, your impression of naturalness.

In the case of convenience, do you want to eat it while traveling to work or at work? Do you need it ready to eat or quick to prepare? What do you mean by quick to prepare? Is it more convenient to prepare it the night before so that it is ready to eat in the morning, or better to prepare it 'fresh' in the morning? Do you want to cook it from scratch, heat it up, or just add hot water (or hot milk)? Some options may be quicker than others but require more attention, while sometimes a slower preparation time may mean you can sort out the kids or get some early work done while your breakfast cooks.

Each option of preparation will also have an impact on your impression of the naturalness of the product.

We are back to the emotional journey – from your choice of oats as a healthier breakfast to the impression you get from the packaging, the look, feel, and aroma of the product, its preparation, its consumption, and the way it makes you feel afterward. Everything about the experience, each small aspect of it, prompts an emotional reaction from you. When the story that you are getting is consistent with your expectations, wants, hopes, and desires, the product works for you. You *believe* that this brand of oats is healthier than your previous breakfast.

Such a belief in a brand may be based on facts – maybe your doctor told you that rolled oats were better for you than highly processed cereals, and you chose the least processed oats that you could find. However, many of the prompts that confirmed these impressions for you may or may not actually be indicators of a better product. Either consciously or unconsciously, you interpreted them to mean something. It is your interpretation of the experience that is important, not whether that experience is genuinely healthier.

As a psychologist working with many great brands and the teams behind them, it often strikes me that while these teams are often completely switched on to the factual benefits and advantages of their brands, they often have little idea about what it is that prompts their consumers to *believe* in these brands. They can wax lyrical about the facts of why their product is 'better' than the competition, but rarely speak about why, or even if, the consumer trusts this story.

Kahneman's System 1 and System 2 thinking helps to explain

Human beings are not logically driven. Nobel laureate Daniel Kahneman explained this beautifully in his book *Thinking, Fast and Slow* (2011). He talks about System 1 and System 2 thinking. System 1 thinking is "fast, instinctive, and emotional", while System 2 is "slower, more deliberate, and logical."

As humans, we respond immediately to stimuli such as advertising, appearance, aroma, taste. We make our connections instantly, instinctively. This is System 1 thinking – emotional. We then back this up with System 2 thinking. We reflect upon our responses and rationalize them.

It takes effort to engage System 2, to rationalize and think logically. Because it takes effort, we don't do it most of the time. When we eat or drink something, we respond to it instinctively. It feels good; it makes us feel better.

However, when you are at work, such emotional responses seem inappropriate. You must stick to the facts, you must be logical and correct about what you say. In my experience, brand owners all too often focus on System 2 and forget that their consumer, when reacting to their product, never leaves System 1. The gap between the two is frequently substantial.

Belief in a brand is an emotional response to the brand experience

We were working for the manufacturer of a leading antacid tablet in the US. It is an incredibly popular antacid, used by millions of Americans every day. As the leading product in its category, it had many competitors vying for consumers' attention, all aiming to be 'better' than our product in some way or another. These proffered more apparently 'modern' formats, 'improved' consumption experiences, and 'better' flavors, while mostly having similar or the same active ingredients and probably the same or similar medical efficacy.

As we profiled the consumer experience of a range of antacids, it became clear that certain things in the experience prompt the consumer to believe in their effectiveness: the way the brand is communicated on the packaging; the appearance and aroma of the tablet or liquid; the feel and aroma in the mouth and particularly in the throat.

Most of these have little relevance to the actual efficacy of the product, but they create a story in the consumer's mind. For some of the products it is a story of reassurance that says this antacid is doing something positive and will make the consumer feel better (a positive reinforcement loop). For others, the story lacks reassurance: It says nothing about the efficacy of the product and does not make them feel better.

This is not about any single key feature; it is about how each stage of the experience builds up to create a comprehensive narrative in the consumer's mind that convinces them of the product's effectiveness. The story reassures them and allows them to stop focusing on their discomfort and to get on with their lives while the antacid is dealing with their discomfort.

Long before any active ingredient can take full effect and do its work, the consumer has already made up their mind about the efficacy of the product. It is not necessarily the best tasting or the most clinically effective product that is preferred, but the one that has the most convincing story in its consumption experience.

Following this work, we were able to create the ideal consumer experience that our client could then orchestrate through their product positioning and communication and through each stage of the consumer use experience. They did not need to have the best taste or the best mouth feel; they just needed to hit the right cues throughout the consumption experience.

The Marketing Clinic has worked on pharmaceutical products, household cleaning products, and personal hygiene products. While their actual efficacy is important, most of the people who choose and use them – you and I – are not scientists and do not have access to the laboratory equipment that would prove that efficacy. As consumers, we rely on proxies that reassure us the product is doing what it is supposed to. How do my teeth feel after using that toothbrush or that brand of toothpaste? How does my kitchen or bathroom look and smell after I have cleaned it?

Whenever we profile these products in use, we always find that, while the consumers will articulate one or two key factors that they say tell them the product is effective, there are, in fact, multiple little prompts that work together to convince the consumer of effectiveness, and only a very few of these are working at a conscious level.

When a brand gets all these little prompts right, it is very powerful, leaving us, the consumers, in no doubt that the product is doing everything we expect of it. We love these products; we truly believe in these brands. This, however, is rare. Most successful brands understand this only on a superficial level. More often there is a wrong turn somewhere in the consumer journey – a slight miscue that does not ring true with the rest of the story the product is telling. We may not be conscious of that miscue, but it undermines our faith in the brand. It makes us more susceptible to trying other brands, to shopping around.

It is these tiny miscues, sometimes multiple miscues, that can be the difference between an average brand and a good one, or between a good brand and a great one.

Why do I choose this brand?

Whether it is a pharmaceutical brand, a household cleaning brand, or a food or drink brand, it should always answer the most important question: "Why do I choose this brand?" The answer is not because you need to relieve pain, to clean, or because you are hungry or thirsty. There are multiple other products out there that can answer these basic requirements. The real question is: "Why do I choose this brand over and above all the alternatives?" Not just the direct competitors, but all the other alternatives that you could have used to satisfy your basic requirement.

If you are buying McVitie's Digestive cookies, why do you choose these above other brands of digestives, or any other cookies? Why do you pick a McVitie's Digestive over and above other snacks, such as potato chips (crisps), chocolate, candy, fruit, nuts, or any of the myriad other things that you could choose to satisfy that urge to have something to eat?

The answer to this question lies in the journey that the McVitie's Digestive takes you on. This journey delivers what you are seeking. If you are consistently choosing McVitie's over and above the alternatives, then clearly, it delivers what you want, at that time, better than any of the alternatives.

This is the core of your faith in the brand. You believe, maybe unconsciously, that McVitie's will deliver what you want, each time. Every time this proves to be true, it confirms your belief in the brand. But if it fails to deliver, this undermines your belief. This is why it is so important that brands really do understand the answer to the question: "Why do people choose my brand?"

Perhaps we should reword the question: "What are the fundamentals of the faith that consumers have in our brand? Why do they believe in us, and how do we honor this faith?"

Why brand extensions often don't work

How often do you see a hugely popular brand that has expanded into a range of flavor or format variants that are OK, but just not as good as the original? People like the original product, it's great, and whenever the brand launches a different flavor it feels quite exciting. But the new flavors never seem quite as good as the original and, after some initial excitement, they seem to disappear quite quickly.

It is unlikely that the format is wrong or that the brand has delivered a dud flavor. There will have been ample research carried out to ensure that it got these right. It is more likely that the brand has missed something in the core of the consumers' belief in the product, that the narrative of the product delivery has slipped, taken a slight wrong turn, and consumers are receiving a small miscue. It's probably very subtle – maybe they are not even consciously aware of it – but this new format or flavor is just not quite delivering as well as the original.

Maybe the original is strawberry flavor and after extensive research the brand team have come out with a lemon flavor. You can be sure that they will have got the flavor intensity and balance right. The lemon will be neither too sweet nor too sour, and it will deliver the same summer flavor and refreshing cues. The team will have tested the new flavor and consumers will have said that it was at least as good as the original, maybe better, and how great it will be to have an alternative flavor.

At first the new flavor sells well. It creates some excitement and a renewed interest in the brand. But then sales quickly tail away. Lots of consumers try it, think it is a great idea, but quickly they find that they are choosing to buy the original again rather than the new flavor.

This is when The Marketing Clinic gets asked to find out what is wrong.

First, we work to understand what it is about the brand, its story, and the product delivery that evoke the belief consumers have in the brand. Then we look at the flavor variant to see how that delivers. It is great - it delivers everything, except for just one or two small miscues.

A good strawberry flavor is quite a complex thing. A balance of sweet and sour, ripe, juicy notes, and sharper - even astringent - green notes. Such complexities tend to be experienced by the consumer mid to rear mouth, later in the consumption experience. Lemon is a much simpler, cleaner flavor. Its sweetness is experienced much earlier in the mouth - right at the start of consumption. Its sourness - making the mouth water and delivering freshness - is also earlier than much of the strawberry experience.

Although the overall sweetness of the product is the same for both versions, the lemon flavor delivers its sweetness right at the beginning of the consumption journey. As is so often the case when companies test their new products with consumers, the greater initial hit of sweetness caused many of those consumers to feel that they preferred the lemon flavor to the strawberry. However, when eaten on its usual occasions, this earlier, sweeter taste, although popular, seemed out of sequence compared to the more complex later strawberry flavor. It gave the wrong cues. It changed the narrative of the product.

The answer could have been a more complex, less initially sweet lemon flavor such as a lemon verbena, but the opportunity has been lost. The consumer has now decided that the lemon version is not for them.

At least after our research the company understood the basis of consumers' belief in its brand. Future, more successful, flavor variants were developed that delivered to this belief rather than undermining it.

The challenge of reducing salt, fat, and sugar

Another of my favorite examples of understanding the consumer's belief in a brand is the reformulation of products to reduce salt, fat, or sugar content.

There is immense pressure on food and drink manufacturers from government, from lobby groups, and also from their consumers to make their products healthier. In most cases that means reducing the salt, fat, or sugar content or overall calorific value.

When producing a food or drink product, much work and research goes into getting the flavor exactly right for the target market. If a product is doing well, it is a good indication that the team have got the flavor, mouth feel, and other aspects just right. When they are then asked to remove some of the fat content, or reduce the amount of sugar or salt, this will not only change the taste but also affect the consistency and mouth feel of the product.

When the brand team taste this product and compare it to the original, it will be quite a disappointment. When they take it out to consumers and ask them how it tastes, the feedback is invariably at least as disappointing as their own assessment. So, even greater efforts go into replacing the lost flavor and mouth feel and getting the 'healthier' product to taste as close to the original version as possible.

In truth, they can never get the reformulated version to be the same as the original, but they get it to be as close as possible and launch it hoping either that the consumer will not notice the difference or that they will be happy to trade a slight loss in satisfaction for the knowledge that this product is better for them.

But this is entirely the wrong approach.

It is true that if you go and ask the consumer what they want, they will tell you that they want the product to taste exactly the same but be healthier. This is a great example of the axiom frequently attributed to Henry Ford (although I can find no proof that he ever actually said it): "If I asked the consumer what they wanted, they would say they wanted a faster horse."

If we, as consumers, are choosing a healthier product, or a brand is offering one, then there needs to be something about the consumption experience of that product that convinces us that this is healthier. Instead of trying to replicate a successful product with a different recipe, companies need to start by understanding why their current product is successful. What is the emotional journey that the product takes the consumer on? What is the mood shift that it delivers and how does it do this? Once this is understood, they need to replicate this emotional journey to deliver the same mood shift as the original product, but along the way we need a slight diversion.

It is like changing your route to work so that it no longer goes past your ex's home. It does not change the start or endpoint, it makes no material change to the journey, but it removes a part of the route that you used to enjoy but that now no longer seems relevant to you. It makes the route more suitable for your revised requirements. Before long, you realize that this is a better route anyway and wonder why you ever liked the original one.

The new product does taste a little different, but that difference confirms for the consumer that it is a healthier version than the original, while the overall consumption experience delivers the same mood shift that they have always enjoyed from the product. If the 'healthier' version tastes the same as the original, it will perform well in preference testing (consumers will say that they like it), but in real life they will not believe it is any different from the original. "Have they really reduced the sugar? Are they trying to trick me?" It undermines their belief and faith in the brand.

The trick is not in minimizing the change in the taste and mouth feel of the product; it is in managing that change to ensure it is delivering the right story to the consumer, that it is consistently building on and never undermining their faith in your brand.

Consider sodas. We all know that they contain more sugar in one can than we should be consuming in a whole day. So we have a choice:

- ¶ we can ignore this fact and enjoy our drink
- ¶ we can avoid sodas altogether
- ¶ or we can drink the no- or low-sugar versions.

Diet Coke tastes different from the full-sugar version. Many will say that it is not as good. However, most consumers of Diet Coke will tell you they prefer it to Coke. They have made a decision not to consume that quantity of sugar. Now, whenever they drink a full-sugar Coke, it tastes inappropriate to them. The knowledge that this is not good for them spoils the experience. The different taste of the diet version feels more appropriate. They believe this to be healthier, better for them. There is nothing inappropriate about drinking Diet Coke, so they can enjoy this drink.

If Diet Coke tasted exactly the same as Coke, there would be nothing about its consumption experience that convinced the consumer that it was any healthier. They would not believe in the diet product. It would not establish a mass faithful following.

The Shape of Taste is a great tool in improving faith and belief in a brand and in adapting, evolving, and improving brands and products. In the next chapter I will look at how these same principles can be used to create new brands and new products that consumers will love.

Key ideas from this chapter

🍴 Human beings are not logically driven.

🍴 It takes effort to engage System 2, to rationalize and think logically. Because it takes effort, we don't do it most of the time. When we eat or drink something, we respond to it instinctively. It feels good; it makes us feel better.

🍴 When you are at work, such emotional responses seem inappropriate: You must stick to the facts; you must be logical and correct about what you say. In my experience, brand owners all too often focus on System 2 and forget that their consumer, when reacting to their product, never leaves System 1 (the immediate emotional response). The gap between the two is frequently substantial.

🍴 Belief in a brand is an emotional response to the brand experience.

🍴 What are the fundamentals of the faith that consumers have in your brand? Why do they believe in it, and how do you honor this faith?

🍴 When changing a recipe, the trick is not in minimizing the change in the taste and mouth feel of the product; it is in managing that change to ensure it is delivering the right story to the consumer, and that it is consistently building on and never undermining their faith in your brand.

Chapter 8

Creating new products that consumers will love

Finding the gaps in the market, the opportunities for new or modified products that satisfy a new or unanswered consumer need, is the aspiration of many brand owners. However, many of these 'gaps' in the market turn out to be holes down which much time, effort, money, and even careers disappear. In this chapter, I show how you can use the principle of the Shape of Taste to help identify opportunities for new products and to create new products and product ranges that meet consumers' emotional needs and so are more likely to succeed.

People love new experiences, new products. Supermarkets love big banners to advertise 'new' lines. We love to tell friends and colleagues about a new product or experience that we have just 'discovered.' They are exciting, they add variety and often improve our lives.

But, in reality, consumers are very cautious about anything new and at least 80 percent of new products do not survive. (Estimates do vary on the failure rate of new products depending upon definitions of a new product and of success and failure.) This can be rooted in a distrust of the unknown, an unconscious bias for the known, safe option rather than the unproven. It may be a nervousness about spending money on, or giving our time to, something that might not be as good as the trusted alternative, of letting ourselves down when others don't like what we have bought for them.

So, companies are cautious about the new lines they offer. It can cost millions to develop and launch a new line, and careers often depend on its success. Most 'new' lines are just a flavor variant or small adaptation of an existing successful product. The Pareto principle applies here: 80 percent familiar and 20 percent new helps everyone to feel comfortable with a familiar product that they know how and when to use with a new and exciting twist that makes it feel different.

If a new product is to be adopted, it must have a strong emotional resonance with the consumer. This is not a rational, logical evaluation of the product advantages against alternatives, but an emotional belief that this will improve your life, or the lives of your family or others close to you. The taste or texture will enhance your enjoyment of it. The new ingredients will benefit your or your loved ones' health. You believe buying this product is better for the environment or local economy, and that will make you feel better about it and about yourself.

Initial attraction and excitement at a concept, even the strongest logical reasoning, is not enough. The consumer has to be attracted on an emotional level; they have to believe it will improve their life.

If a new fruit juice has reduced sugar and 50 percent fewer calories, or a new yogurt contains more strawberries and has an 'improved flavor', these are unlikely to motivate consumers in themselves. Motivation to purchase and to then keep purchasing is far more likely if they believe that the fruit juice will help them to lose weight or will save their children's teeth from decaying, or that their family will love the strawberries in their yogurt and appreciate them for buying it.

Understanding the consumers' emotional requirements and how these can be met through the brand and product experience is key.

Identifying and meeting emotional requirements

I hope I have established in your mind by now that every consumer experience results in an emotional journey. It changes the consumer's mood in some way. This mood shift is never a simple switch from mood A to mood B. Your brand experience takes your consumer on a journey from A to B via X, Y, and Z on the way. And as I have already said, while the endpoint is important, it's the journey that is the essence of the brand.

Identifying emotional journeys that resonate with your consumers and how to deliver these journeys through product and communications development is the key to developing successful new products and improving upon existing ones.

Whether you are seeking the next great innovation or just trying to steal a march on the competition, delivering great emotional journeys through well-planned and well-understood brand experiences will not only give you the edge, it will also leave your competition wondering what happened.

Developing the Walkers Deli range

In 2012, Walkers (part of PepsiCo) asked The Marketing Clinic to help them develop a new range of potato chips for the UK. The brand had identified a market of slightly older consumers who loved potato chips and were looking for more premium products but preferred familiar deli flavors to the more exotic international flavors usually associated with the Walkers Sensations range.

Walkers had put together a team of talented development chefs and come up with a range of established deli flavors that they thought would translate well into potato chips. Each chef had developed their own versions of various classic recipes. The problem was which version of each recipe Walkers should use, and how to measure if the flavor journey was being delivered in the right way when translated into a chip flavor. The question was not, "Whose version of Ham Hock with Mature Cheddar and Farmhouse Chutney was the best?" but, "What is the emotional journey we need to deliver and which recipe delivers it most accurately?"

We spent a wonderful couple of days in a development kitchen somewhere in the Midlands of England, with the chefs creating their best dishes and us profiling them with ordinary target consumers. The question was never to ask which ones they preferred, but to identify the taste and emotional journeys that each recipe delivered and to map out the consumers' responses. By the end of two days, we could show exactly what the ideal emotional journey was for the range to deliver, how this could be delivered with a target Shape of Taste for the brand, and how each recipe that had been developed matched or varied from this ideal Shape of Taste.

We were able to write taste briefs for each flavor variant, pick the recipes that best matched these, and make recommendations regarding how they could be adapted to get an even closer match to the ideal.

Armed with this information, the flavor developers were able to go away and create a first pass of each flavor as a potato chip. A couple of months later, we then profiled these chips with consumers to check their match to the ideal in terms of both the taste journey delivered and, more importantly, the emotional journey. We then passed our development notes on to the flavor team to further improve the offerings.

Walkers Market Deli chips were launched in late 2013 and are a highly successful addition to the Walkers range. If you are in the UK, give them a try and see what you think.

More than just a Milky Way

When looking to develop new products, companies rarely start from scratch. As mentioned at the beginning of this chapter, it is usual for new products to be variants of an existing product.

When you understand how the consumption journey evokes the mood shift, you really begin to understand your food and drink and can look at how you might produce the same mood shift, the same brand essence, via a different category altogether.

When manufacturers see their brands purely in product terms, e.g. it is a chocolate bar, they find themselves restricted to flavor variants and size changes. If, however, they can articulate exactly the mood shift that a brand delivers, they can start to imagine how else to deliver that same mood shift with different product types.

There may be some elements of the consumption journey – even some that are quite significant and noticeable – that have little or no relevance to the mood shift. These are attributes that can be changed, probably within certain parameters, without affecting the critical mood shift.

Once you become aware of the textural and taste characteristics that you can change while still delivering the desired mood shift, this creates opportunities for some very creative brand extensions that can take the brand – and everything that it means to the consumer – into completely new areas. In the UK, Mars, for example, is not just a chocolate bar but delivers its same mood shift through ice cream, drinks, and cakes. These product variants seem obvious now, but only became so when Mars started to think differently about what the Milky Way delivered.

Others have tried to follow such diversification but have not always been successful when they have not fully understood that it is the mood shift that is important and what needs to be replicated in the new category.

Creating new opportunities in East and Southern Africa

Another way to use the Shape of Taste as a route for creating new products is to start by identifying emotional journeys that the consumer would like but are not currently available and create products that meet these unfulfilled needs.

The East and Southern Africa Region (ESAR) at Nestlé has 23 countries and a population of about 470 million. This is comparable to the Central and West Africa Region (CWAR) in terms of population but is significantly smaller in terms of sales. It is believed that an important factor in this difference is that CWAR has one or two key products that drive a more intense interest in Nestlé as a whole at a trade level.

The Marketing Clinic was asked by Nestlé to identify a new opportunity for which they could develop a new product or range of products – one that would create more interest in Nestlé across the 23 ESAR markets and thus drive significant growth in the region as a whole. In order to succeed quickly, the product needed to match an existing need, but not have any immediate competitors. It needed to appear new and exciting while also slotting immediately into consumers' lives across all 23 different markets.

Identifying the best product to drive growth is not just about identifying a product that consumers 'like.' For it to succeed, the product must answer a real need in the consumers' lives. This need may be currently unrecognized, or it may be satisfied by something else. In either case we were asking consumers to change their behavior.

Behavior changes are rarely rational. If the current behavior has worked so far, there is no rational reason to change it. Instead, these behavior changes tend to be emotionally driven: "It feels more modern," or, "Everyone else is using these now," and, "It will improve our lives..." And this emotional driver must be strong enough to overcome the natural and cultural conservatism that will resist such a change. Just because a consumer 'likes' a concept or a product, it doesn't mean they will change their established behavior and buy it on a regular basis.

To understand and identify the potential products for this project, we needed to understand the emotional drivers of our consumers, how current products and behaviors met their needs, the potential gaps, and how our products could be seen to fit into these spaces.

By examining consumers' emotional and rational needs across the region, we identified a new opportunity with a keenly focused product range that had immense emotional appeal to consumers throughout the ESAR markets – a range that immediately resonated with consumers yet had limited competition. Consumers were able immediately to identify how the brand fit into and improved their lives and those of their families.

While the range was strongly endorsed by the Nestlé brand, it also promoted and strengthened the brand in all these markets. We were also able to recommend to the team a cross-region positioning and emotive communications for the new brand and how they needed to adapt these to maximize success in each individual market.

The examples in this chapter show how an understanding of the Shape of Taste is very helpful in updating existing brands and products and in creating new ones. In the next chapter, I will look at how it helps in understanding and adapting to the way different cultures in different markets mean that consumers often respond differently to the same brands and products.

Key ideas from this chapter

🍴 If a new product is to be adopted, it must have a strong emotional resonance with the consumer. They must believe this product will improve their life in some way.

🍴 This is not a rational, logical evaluation of the product advantages against alternatives, but an emotional belief that this will improve your life, or the lives of your family or others close to you.

🍴 Understanding the consumers' emotional requirements and how these can be met through the brand and product experience is key.

🍴 Whether you are seeking the next great innovation or just trying to steal a march on the competition, delivering great emotional journeys through well-planned and well-understood brand experiences will not only give you the edge, it will also leave your competition wondering what happened.

🍴 The question should not be, "Whose version of Ham Hock with Mature Cheddar and Farmhouse Chutney is the best?" but, "What is the emotional journey we need to deliver and which recipe delivers it most accurately?"

🍴 When you understand how the consumption journey evokes the mood shift, you really begin to understand your food and drink and can look at how you might produce the same mood shift, the same brand essence, via a different category altogether.

🍴 When manufacturers see their brands purely in product terms, e.g. it is a chocolate bar, they find themselves restricted to flavor variants and size changes. If, however, they can articulate exactly the mood shift that a brand delivers they can start to imagine how else to deliver that same mood shift with different product types.

¶ Once you become aware of the textural and taste characteristics that you can change while still delivering the desired mood shift, this creates opportunities for some very creative brand extensions that can take the brand, and everything that it means to the consumer, into completely new areas.

¶ Behavior changes are rarely rational. If the current behavior has worked so far, there is no rational reason to change it. Instead, these behavior changes tend to be emotionally driven.

Chapter 9

Cultural understanding is important... but cultures are not static

It is obvious to anyone who has ever traveled outside their hometown that, like accents and language, food cultures vary with geography. I grew up in the 1970s in the south-east of England and then spent the first ten years of my working life in Yorkshire in the north of England. In Yorkshire, I made many friends and was very happy, but I was always an outsider. Not only did I talk with a funny southern English accent, I also had strange food habits, such as preferring fresh (or frozen) garden peas over proper mushy marrowfat peas. I ate my pork pies cold and without gravy, I never ordered 'scraps' with my fish and chips, and had no idea what a breadcake was (I had always called them bread rolls).

Different cultures have different food and drink traditions and consumers in different markets have different expectations. This means that the consumer responses to the same product may well vary in different markets. In this chapter, you will discover how the Shape of Taste can be used to explain and understand these variations and help brand owners to adapt their products and communications to suit different cultures.

I don't think I have ever visited a country, or even a region, that is not proud of its own food heritage. It is true that, as more people travel and more frequently, and as food companies become increasingly global, many of these differences seem to shrink in significance. There will be a McDonald's and a Starbucks almost anywhere you go. Coca-Cola, Pepsi, and Nescafé are almost ubiquitous. But while the globe may be said to be shrinking, while people relocate around our planet and many cultures absorb bits of other cultures, there remain strong regional and national differences within and between markets. These make food and drink a fantastic part of any travel experience but, at the same time, often one of the more difficult things to cope with if you relocate. It also creates opportunities and difficulties for any food or drink company hoping to trade across borders.

Nescafé is one of the most well-known coffee brands across the globe and is the leading instant coffee brand in practically every market in which it operates. But it is not the same product in each market. The Nescafé team are constantly vigilant to changing tastes between and within markets, adjusting their formulae to best suit the requirements of each particular market at any particular time.

McDonald's, that icon of American food culture exported around the globe, also varies not only its menu offering and the range of sauces and dips, but even the contents and presentation of its iconic burgers. In the Philippines, the bun is often substituted with steamed rice formed into a bun shape. In China, all the chicken burgers use premium thigh meat rather than the breast preferred in Western markets, while the salad content is increased, is more visible, and has greater emphasis in all the pictures, reflecting the greater emphasis in China on including their four food types (grains, vegetables, fruit, and meat) in each meal. In India, McDonald's serves no beef at all and burgers are either chicken or aloo (a spiced potato and pea patty covered in breadcrumbs).

As brands spread across markets, they need to be conscious not only of how their positioning and communications need to be varied, but also how people in different cultures will respond differently to the consumption experience of their products. It is not just about offering different flavors or different formats to suit the requirements of different markets – it is about understanding the emotional journey that the product evokes for the consumer and how the same consumption journey may evoke quite a different emotional reaction in different markets.

Sometimes the differences are obvious and easy to understand. In America, peanuts and peanut flavors are widely popular. Peanut butter is an American icon enjoyed by children and adults alike and is incorporated into confectionery, food, and cooking. In China, peanuts are peasants' food, old fashioned and, in a rapidly urbanizing society, of the countryside. They cheapen any food product that they are added to, making it generally less aspirational, less attractive.

At other times, the differences are more deeply buried – less obvious to the observer, harder to understand. It is clear that consumers in market A are responding differently to the same product than those in market B, but unless the company can understand why this is the case and what it is about the product experience that prompts the different reaction, it will not know how it should adapt to this difference. Does it change the advertising? Does it change the product formula, and if so, how? Or is the difference in the consumer reaction not, in fact, important and does it just carry on regardless?

In Chapter 3, I discussed the different emotional cues that drive feelings of premiumness for Nescafé in China and in the Philippines (see pages 53-4). Understanding such subtle variances between markets is important for the positioning and communication of a brand. It is these subtle differences that can determine success or failure in different markets.

The significance of face creams in Brazil

I came across a different example of the importance of understanding cultural differences when I was researching women's face creams in Brazil. The client was an international pharmaceutical company and the face cream team were based in the UK.

As is often the case when researching cosmetics, we asked the women to come in to our research group without any cream or makeup on their face. To ask women who are regular users of makeup to turn up to a group without any is often challenging in any country. To ask Brazilian women to arrive without any makeup and without applying any face cream that morning was especially so.

While we got the participants to try some creams and profiled their experiences, we also prompted and listened to their stories about why it was so difficult for them to come out without their makeup and why their face creams were so important to them. The stories were much the same as we might hear in any market – about how important it was that they always look their best, about how their skin wasn't what it used to be when they were younger, and how they didn't like what the years were doing to their faces. But what was chilling to my naive English ears was the undercurrent of abject fear that if they lost their looks, their husbands would leave them and find a younger, more attractive woman.

Yes, this is not a unique sentiment and it has come up occasionally in groups in many places over the years. But here it was a consistent theme and never joked about. Once the topic was raised, the shared concern and mutual understanding among every group was tangible. The importance of the face cream for these Brazilian women, in their minds, was a matter of maintaining not just their looks but their marriages and everything that they had and were.

As I articulated this back in London to an almost entirely female Anglo-Saxon audience, it seemed a little extreme.

"Really?" they said. "Is this true?" They turned to the one other male in the room: a very pleasant, well-liked, and reasonably senior member of the team who happened to be a Brazilian man, probably in his late thirties.

"Oh yes," he said, entirely matter of factly. "I am on my second wife now and she is younger than my first."

From Italian taste preferences to double dipping

A few years ago, I stumbled upon a great example of how a subtle difference, driven more by geography than by culture, resulted in a massive difference in taste preferences. I was researching the optimum taste profile for an iced tea brand in Italy. Many researchers would do this by offering subtly different versions of their drink to consumers and evaluating their responses, adjusting the levels of flavor, sweetness, and sourness until they had a drink preferred by the greatest number of respondents.

It works if you are looking for incremental improvements to existing products, but in this case the client was aiming to drive a step change in the market. To do that we started by determining the emotional journey that the consumers were seeking when choosing iced tea and then established the best consumption experience to deliver that emotional mood shift. Surprisingly, this is often not as complicated or as drawn out as the traditional process, because once we have established the emotional requirements, we can move quickly to the ideal taste profile without all the trial-and-error iterations.

I started by understanding what our respondents drank as young children. Water, they all said. A certain amount of fruit juice and some Coke, Pepsi, or other carbonated drinks now and then at special occasions, but the norm was water.

When we tracked the evolution of their taste palates as they got older, it was clear to me that something was missing. There was a disconnect between drinking water for refreshment as a child and the simple, clean, but strong flavors of Italian cuisine. Put simply, it did not make sense that a nation that drank water for refreshment as children would move on to espressos. As I searched for what was missing, I went back to the start:

Me:	What did you drink as a child?
Respondent:	Water.
Me:	Who prepared the water for you?
Respondent:	Well, my mom usually.
Me:	Tell me how your mom prepared a glass of water for you.
Respondent:	(What an odd question.) Well, she got a glass, added water from the tap, and squeezed in some lemon.
Me:	Ah. So where did Mom get the lemon from?
Respondent:	Well, the tree in the garden of course (where else do you get lemons from?).
Me:	So did Mom always put lemon in your water?
Respondent:	Of course.
Me:	And when you got your own water did you put lemon in it?
Respondent:	Yes, of course. Who drinks water without lemon in it?

I may exaggerate slightly, but as we explored what our respondents really drank as children, it was not water, but water with lemon in it – and often quite a good amount of lemon too, not just a light squeeze. What is more, in many cases, these lemons were either from the tree in their garden or locally grown, so probably sharper and less sweet than many commercially grown lemons.

That there was lemon in the water was such a normal, accepted fact that it had not occurred to anyone that they should point it out. However, it was the missing link. From a very young age (from as early as they could remember), if they were thirsty, if they needed refreshment, they would drink water with a good dash of quite sour lemon. Not the bland, subtle refreshment of plain water but the definite, clean, clear taste of fresh lemon. Now the evolution of the Italian taste palate through the simple, clean, fresh flavors of Italian cuisine to their love of the espresso made sense.

Aside from the difference that this made to how our client flavored their iced tea, this also got me thinking about a few comparisons around the world.

As a child in England in the 1970s, the standard drink for my generation was fruit squash. Orange was my favorite, but lemon was just as popular. Water was boring, we never wanted to drink just water, but fruit squash made it much more interesting and, probably even more important, it added sweetness. But in most cases, that sweetness came from neither the fruit nor from sugar; it came from artificial sweeteners.

These fruit squashes are something of a UK phenomenon. I have not come across them to any great extent in any other market. So, my generation and others before and after me in the UK were raised acquiring a taste for artificial sweeteners in a way that does not happen in other markets. Does this explain why diet drinks, with their distinctive tang of artificial sweeteners, are so much more successful in the UK than in other markets?

In Southeast Asia there is a strong culture of sharing food. Yes, in most cultures we share food, but in Asia the culture of sharing is deeply ingrained. Snacks will be pooled and shared by the group; meals typically comprise various dishes that are shared by everyone present. Food is taken from the communal dish in small quantities not just once but repeatedly throughout the meal.

Anglo-Saxon cultures tend to be more self-focused about food. Snacks are more personal, shared reluctantly if politeness requires it. Meals may be served from a communal dish, but only once at the beginning of a meal. While the Chinese and many other cultures find great pleasure in sharing their food, our research shows that Americans – in particular, but us Brits increasingly too – are becoming more and more selfish about our food and particularly about the apparent horrors of double dipping!

Cultures are never static

That brands must be aware of cultural and market differences should be self-evident to any international marketer, but cultures are never static. Consumers and the markets that they create constantly move forward and they often leave us behind as they do.

When I first visited China, I found a rapidly moving, modernizing market. Things were changing fast, as they still are. But there were cultural, political, and ethnographical differences that meant the Chinese market was never just going to follow Western markets. It was generally accepted that there were certain truisms that would never change. One was that everybody drank tea and this was not a market that was going to drink much coffee. We have already seen how true that turned out to be in Chapter 3 (see pages 51–3). Another was that the Chinese did not like dairy products, that in fact many Chinese are intolerant of dairy, and there was little point in anyone trying to promote milk, yogurt, or cheese in China.

Now, however, China is one of the most dynamic and rapidly growing dairy markets in the world as these products are viewed as important modern health products. It is increasingly popular to encourage children to drink milk and yogurt to help them grow and learn and prestigious for teens and adults to be seen consuming and enjoying dairy products.

Accepted views and stereotypes must always be challenged as marketers expand the markets for their products. While riding roughshod over cultures and traditions will never benefit anyone, they are rarely the block to innovation and expansion that they are often perceived to be. It is important to be able to see and understand these traditions and cultural references from the perspective of the consumer in that market today. But, maybe surprisingly, it often takes an outsider to recognize a change in attitudes and be able to articulate them in a way that the local marketers can then respond to. This was the case when we were brought in to research UHT milk for Nestlé Pakistan.

Listening to consumers: UHT milk in Pakistan

In order to understand anything about the milk market in Pakistan, first you need to understand the traditional production and distribution system. Many rural families will own a few buffalo, cows, or goats. They collect the milk from their own animals and take it to a central point in their village, where it is all tipped into one communal container: all the milk from the buffalo, cows, and goats, all mixed together. Then along comes a collection truck that tours the local villages and the milk is transported to the appropriate urban center. From here it is then distributed to the retail outlets.

I hope you have been paying attention because at no point did I mention cold chain or temperature control. The daytime temperature could be 40° Celsius, but there is little or no temperature-controlled distribution. Although, in recognition of this fact, the collection truck will often be loaded up with ice before it sets out to help keep the milk cool. Yes, the tank contains a load of frozen water to which the milk is added.

It is a traditional part of the Pakistani family routine that the wife or mother rises early before the rest of the household and goes out to purchase the day's milk. She carries this home and the first thing she must do is boil it all in order to sterilize it and ensure that it will last the day. She will then divide the milk into various pots and containers for the different functions for which it will be needed that day. Now it is time to wake the kids and get them ready for school.

One of the ways in which a new wife shows her love and commitment to the family is when she takes over this task from her new mother-in-law. It is important that the first glasses of warm milk are ready for her husband's first cup of tea when he gets up and for the children to drink before they set off for school. So when a researcher calls round to ask about her experience, likes, and dislikes about milk in her life, the universal answer is to discuss her frustration and mistrust of the supply chain. You never know what you are getting, how much buffalo milk is in the mix, how much cow's and goat's. How much has it been diluted by the ice? How creamy or watery will it be? How much has the milk begun to sour before I can boil it?

This variability can be critical, as it affects the quality of the tea that is made with the milk – and we knew from a previous project in Pakistan that a wife's ability to make tea in just the right way is very important.

It took much more artful questioning and a much longer route around the subject for the women to talk about the process of collecting, boiling, and dividing the milk every morning. Tradition is strong in Pakistan; expectations are passed down the generations. To confess that they would rather stay in bed a little longer and not have to do this was akin to confessing to being a bad wife, mother, and daughter-in-law, to the evading of their responsibilities.

Nestlé and other organizations, however, did offer an alternative. They had modern collection systems collecting from identified farms with consistent cold chain and they sterilized the milk, offering cartons of consistent UHT milk. This UHT milk relieved the young wife or mother of the burden of rising early to buy, boil, and sort the milk and gave her the consistency of quality and taste that she required. But, in the eyes of the matriarchal mother-in-law, such motivations were a shirking of a traditional responsibility. No daughter-in-law of theirs would make such a move. However, when UHT milk is presented as a positive health benefit for the children and for the rest of the family, the same matriarch would expect any responsible daughter-in-law who loved and cared for her family to make this now-important switch.

These insights emerged and were consistently endorsed as we researched in different, more and less traditional locations around Pakistan. Along with our findings around the ideal taste profile and how this differentiated the Nestlé milk from its competitors, these insights were creating some excitement among the marketers who were traveling with us. It was also becoming clear that, while the market opportunity was perhaps greater than they had realized, their communications strategy also needed to be adjusted to convey Nestlé's specific advantages over and above other UHT milks and so take a greater share of the growing market, rather than just grow the market for all.

But I got my greatest surprise when we presented these findings to the dairy team back in Lahore. The group ranged from board level to marketing and brand managers to product developers. As I explained the housewives' frustration at the quality and variability of the milk supply chain, we saw many sage nods around the room: "Yes, it was terrible." But when I explained how they hated the collecting, boiling, and dividing of the milk, I was challenged. Had we misunderstood them? Surely this was an important part of a wife and mother's duty to her family? It is an old tradition; Pakistan is a strongly traditional society. Were we imposing our Western views on something we did not understand?

The males in the room looked to their female compatriots, who smiled and said, "No they are absolutely right. We have been waiting for someone to explain this for a while, but local researchers have never really cracked it."

This was one of those moments when I know why I love this job that I have. Faces change, lights go on, and you can see strategies begin to transform in front of your eyes.

Key ideas from this chapter

🍴 As brands spread across markets, they need to be conscious not only of how their positioning and communications need to be varied, but also how people in different cultures will respond differently to the consumption experience of their products.

🍴 The same consumption journey (the same taste and texture) may evoke quite a different emotional reaction in different markets.

🍴 That brands must be aware of cultural and market differences should be self-evident to any international marketer, but cultures are never static. Consumers and the markets that they create constantly move forward and they often leave us behind as they do.

🍴 While riding roughshod over cultures and traditions will never benefit anyone, they are rarely the block to innovation and expansion that they are often perceived to be.

🍴 Faces change, lights go on, and you can see strategies begin to transform in front of your eyes.

Chapter 10

Telling stories that product owners may not want to hear

Most of the time my colleagues at The Marketing Clinic and I can go back to a client and give them the answers they are seeking: That this is the best way to design or communicate their new product; that with these clear adjustments they can overcome the new competitive challenge. We can show them why they have been struggling with a particular issue and how they can change their approach to overcome their problem.

But sometimes it is not that straightforward. Even when we are going back to our clients with the answers to their questions, there is a part of our findings that will not be so welcome. Most clients take it well. The point of doing market research is to learn, to be better informed, to make better decisions, to avoid making costly mistakes. But we are all human and to be told that you have made a mistake, that you have been heading off in the wrong direction, or that your new product is not going to work, can be quite a blow. Individuals also sometimes need convincing that our research is correct. They know their products, they know their markets, and they have data and other research that led them to make the decisions that they have so far.

But when, in our debriefs, we take the client through the

Shape of Taste – when we walk them through how and why their communications and the sensorial experience of the product prompts the consumers' emotional responses – then our clients generally understand what is going wrong. More importantly, they also realize what they need to do about it – normally, before we get round to pointing this out to them.

This chapter shares some cases where we knew that we had to tell the client something they might not be prepared to hear. I will show that when the research is solid and well explained, and once the client understands their Shape of Taste, they start to see for themselves what needs fixing and how to fix it. These examples also show that if you are honest about your findings, giving the client the whole truth and not just the bits you think they will be pleased with, everyone profits in the end.

When we arrived in Pakistan to help out on UHT milk (see pages 117-9 in the previous chapter), one of the first things we were shown was a fantastic new advertising campaign that had just been launched. The team were justifiably proud of it. This was a beautiful campaign – creative, wonderfully executed, and it showed the product off well.

Two weeks later, after doing our work, we recognized that this campaign was going to help Nestlé's competitors as much as it helped them. Part of our debrief had to show our clients this, and how and why they had to change their messaging if they were to regain market share. Recalling how proudly the marketing director had shown us the new ads, I was a little nervous about how this would go down.

But as we presented the Shapes of Taste for their UHT milk and highlighted the similarities and competitive differences between their taste curves and those of their competitors, that same marketing director spoke up from the back of the room: "We are going to have to change our campaign, aren't we? We are growing the market rather than our share."

Explaining the mood shift for
Walkers Sensations and Pringles

When Walkers launched Sensations in the UK, the range completely revolutionized the premium and adult potato chip market and their competitors were forced to react. We were approached by P&G who, at that time, owned Pringles. The brand team had had a good look at Sensations, their more sophisticated flavors, their adult packaging, their positioning, and the way they described and depicted all of this on the pack and in their advertising.

Pringles had developed its own series of more adult, sophisticated flavors and some well-written flavor descriptions and marketing messages. As you would expect from a billion-dollar brand owned by a company like P&G, these were all good. What they wanted from us was to test the different flavors against Sensations and other competitors and tell them which they should launch first, which were also good to go but later, and which needed some more work.

As we profiled the products with consumers and understood the emotional journeys they delivered, and as we built an understanding of the Shape of Taste that Sensations potato chips were delivering and why this had shaken up the market, we also began to realize that the new Pringles flavors were just that. They were flavor variants of Pringles. They delivered essentially the same Shape of Taste that Pringles had always delivered. This was not the new, more exciting experience that Sensations were eliciting. They were great Pringles flavors, but they were not going to compete with Sensations. This, we recognized, was not going to be good news when we delivered it to our client. They needed to respond to this new threat and were ready to launch once we told them which to go with.

We started our debrief by showing the client exactly what Sensations delivered in terms of the emotional journey, how this was different from other potato chips and from

Pringles, and explaining why this was important and why it had transformed the market. We then showed them how Sensations delivered this emotional journey through their sensorial journey: we took them through the Shape of Taste.

We were then about to move on to how the new Pringles flavors worked, but before we did so the development director leading the project spoke up: "Our flavors are not going to do that, are they? We thought it was the flavor choices and descriptions that made the difference, but now I can see it is in the sensory journey. I think we need to go away and look at this again, don't we?"

A great cheese brand in the UK

Another example of being very unsure how our findings would be received was when we were asked to work on a cheese brand in the UK. Our recommendations were to move in precisely the opposite direction from the one in which the brand had already started to move.

The UK cheddar cheese market is dominated by supermarket own-label cheeses, with a relatively small number of brands competing for a share. The brand we were working with had been doing well, taking increasing share, and had secured significant shelf space in all the major supermarkets. However, there was a limit to how much more share it could take and, if it was to continue to grow the brand, the company needed to expand it into different products and maybe even beyond cheddar.

The trouble was that the team didn't really know what it was about their cheese that made it so successful and what any brand extensions should look or taste like. They knew their cheese had a 'smoother' taste than competitors' cheeses and communicating this had been an important part of their progress so far, but how did they take this 'smoother' taste into brand extensions?

We profiled the cheese alongside its competitors, mapping

their Shapes of Taste and detailing the sensorial and the emotional journeys. We worked to understand exactly how the sensorial journey produced the consumer's emotional journey, exactly which features prompted what responses and why, the order and intensity of the emotional responses, and how the story came together to produce the consumer's overall reaction to the cheese.

The product was a mature cheddar cheese. Once we could see what it was about the cheese that was really working for consumers and why – once we really understood its Shape of Taste – it was clear to us that the brand extension opportunities were in the direction of mild cheddars and children's products. We prepared our debrief explaining why this was the case.

This, however, left me with one outstanding issue: The company already had an extra mature brand extension. Knowing what I now knew, this made little sense to me. I would never have recommended it, but it was out there on the shelves, and I had no idea how well it was selling.

We structured the debrief to explain the Shape of Taste first, to show the client the emotional journey that its consumers experienced and how and why this was prompted by the specific features of the product. The debrief then went on to show the recommended routes forward, detail the emotional journeys that would be the most effective for the brand extensions, and show how the team could structure their product features and communications to evoke these journeys. It would tell them what we had found and make our recommendations. We would discuss the extra mature issue when it came up.

Well, of course, it did come up, but it required no discussion. As I finished explaining the consumers' sensorial and emotional journeys with their current product, the marketing director piped up: "So that is why the extra mature product isn't doing very well – we need to move towards the mild products, don't we?" The rest of the debrief went very smoothly.

These are not isolated examples. Once the client understands the Shape of Taste connecting the sensorial journey of their product with the emotional journey of the consumer, they see their product in a completely different way.

Dealing with a more difficult response

However, just once in all the years I have been doing this work, I encountered a more difficult situation. We had been researching for a big global brand across three continents. We came back to the debrief with comprehensive recommendations regarding defending its market-leading position against global and local competitors, about future product development directions, and about the brand's communications.

Most of this went down well and the debrief was progressing positively. However, as we spoke about the details of consumers' emotional reactions to the product and how these had implications for the communications strategy, the communications team in the room were not happy.

Until this point, we had not seen the global campaign that they were planning, but now they decided to show it to us. In light of the research that we were debriefing, this campaign promoted a category benefit – something that consumers could attribute to their product but equally to their competitors. I recommended some subtle changes that, while retaining the core creative idea, could nuance the campaign to focus on their specific advantage.

My suggestions were dismissed as irrelevant: The campaign was going to be run as it was. I was happy to defend The Marketing Clinic's findings and point out what I thought were their implications, but it was not my role to argue that the brand should pull or run its campaign. Half the room, however, did think the campaign should be changed and argued strongly that the communications team should listen, while the comms team animatedly defended their campaign. Too much work had been done and they were not changing it now. We were in southern Europe and the discussion got quite animated.

As the brand director walked us out to our taxi back to the airport, it was clear that further internal discussions would have to take place. It was six months later when I received his call: "Do you mind coming back in and presenting your findings again? We have made some changes in the team and it would be very helpful if you could take us through them afresh."

Key ideas from this chapter

🍴 The point of doing market research is to learn, to be better informed, to make better decisions, to avoid making costly mistakes.

🍴 Once the client understands the Shape of Taste connecting the sensorial journey of their product with the emotional journey of the consumer, they see their product in a completely different way.

The value of the Shape of Taste

I hope by now you have recognized that the Shape of Taste is not only a great tool for understanding food and beverage brands and products but also a different approach to thinking about food and drink.

People's love of their food and drink is not based just on the best taste; it is about how these foods make them feel. The preparation, cooking, appearance, aroma, taste of the product itself: Every touchpoint contributes to a profound shift in their mood. The Shape of Taste is an approach to help you understand this mood shift and, more importantly, how and why your food and drinks generate it.

It helps you to create a story in the consumer's mind. It may be a story of love, of reassurance; it may be a story of better nutrition, or one of stimulation or relaxation.

This is not about individual product features. It is about how each stage of the product experience comes together to create a comprehensive narrative in the consumer's mind – a narrative that makes them feel good about consuming your food, that makes them feel good about a brand.

When the consumer believes in a product, when they believe that it is working for them, it makes them feel better and they are motivated to keep using it. This is an emotional rather than a rational reaction.

Understanding consumers' emotional responses and connecting them with the product experience is the advantage that the Shape of Taste brings. When you see your food and drink in this way you can deliver a consumer experience that differentiates you from your competitors and builds the essential belief in your brands, driving liking, preference, loyalty, and advocacy.

How can you make use of the Shape of Taste?

If you work in the food and beverage industry, the Shape of Taste gives you powerful insights into why your consumers respond as they do to your products and how you can adapt your communications and products to evoke even more positive responses.

If food and drink is not your profession but you are interested in how and why you, your family, or friends respond as they do to what they eat and drink, then it gives you a useful framework to explore this with. Hopefully some of the case studies that I have used will help you in this.

When you focus on the emotional journeys that food and drinks generate, rather than on the flavor itself, you start to think about foods differently. You start to see flavor, taste, texture, and communication as the tools that are used to generate the emotional journey rather than as ends in themselves.

You also might start to think differently about why you personally like certain foods, flavors, and textures, and what your underlying motivations are for those meals, snacks, and drinks that you find yourself wanting.

If you are involved in the food and beverage industry, if you find yourself thinking more deeply about your own underlying motivations and food and drink desires, you may also realize how powerful such an understanding is when you can develop it for your brands and product ranges.

At The Marketing Clinic, we are engaged by clients in large and small companies from markets around the world to help with all sorts of food and beverage projects:

- 🍴 identifying new spaces for innovative brands and products
- 🍴 developing and refining new concepts and new products
- 🍴 future-proofing market-leading brands
- 🍴 creating new challenger brands
- 🍴 expanding existing products into new spaces and new markets
- 🍴 improving existing products and communications – dealing with competitive and other market threats.

We also work with companies on a consultative basis to change the focus of their teams from a product focus to identifying and meeting the emotional needs of their consumers.

At the beginning of this book, I asked for your thoughts. I would be a poor researcher if I thought asking this before you had read the book was the best place to do so. Now that you have finished reading, I would love to hear which parts of the book you found most interesting or helpful. Please let me know what you think, or if you would like to know more about the work that we do at The Marketing Clinic.

Thank you

chris@marketingclinic.com

Bibliography

Chapter 1

Anderson, O W (1955) 'Infant feeding and emotional security'. *Hospital Topics*. URL: doi.org/10.1080/00185868.1955.9953550

Cowart, B J (1981) 'Development of taste perception in humans: Sensitivity and preference throughout the life span'. *Psychological Bulletin*. URL: doi.org/10.1037/0033-2909.90.1.43

De Houwer, J, Thomas, S & Baeyens, F (2001) 'Associative learning of likes and dislikes: A review of 25 years of research on human evaluative conditioning'. *Psychological Bulletin*. URL: doi.org/10.1037/0033-2909.127.6.853

Spahn, J M, Callahan E H et al (2019) 'Influence of maternal diet on flavor transfer to amniotic fluid and breast milk and children's responses: A systematic review'. *The American Journal of Clinical Nutrition*. URL: doi.org/10.1093/ajcn/nqy240

Ustun, B, Reissland, N et al (2022) 'Flavor sensing in utero and emerging discriminative behaviors in the human fetus'. *Psychological Science*. URL: doi.org/10.1177/09567976221105460

Chapter 5

Ridder, M (2023) 'Energy drinks market in the UK – statistics & facts'. URL: statista.com/topics/11676/energy-drinks-in-the-united-kingdom/#topicOverview

Collings, V B (1974) 'Human taste response as a function of locus of stimulation on the tongue and soft palate'. *Perception & Psychophysics 16*. URL: doi:10.3758/bf03203270

Chapter 7

Kahneman, D (2011) *Thinking, Fast and Slow*. Penguin.

EU Safety Representative: euComply OÜ Pärnu mnt 139b-14 11317 Tallinn
Estonia hello@eucompliancepartner.com +33 756 90241

www.ingramcontent.com/pod-product-compliance
Lightning Source LLC
Chambersburg PA
CBHW042121190326
41519CB00031B/7570